# THE ABINGDON WOMEN'S PREACHING ANNUAL

Series 1

Year B

COMPILED AND EDITED BY

*Jana L. Childers and Lucy A. Rose*

*Grace and peace —
To my colleague and
mentor in
Spirituality and
Dance.
Lucy*

Abingdon Press
Nashville

THE ABINGDON WOMEN'S PREACHING ANNUAL

Copyright © 1996 by Abingdon Press

This book is printed on recycled, acid-free paper.

ISBN 0-687-00224-9
ISSN 1086-8240

Scripture quotations, unless otherwise indicated, are from the New Revised Standard Version
Bible, copyright © 1989, by the Division of Christian Education of the National Council of the
Churches of Christ in the United States of America.

Scripture quotations noted NIV are taken from the Holy Bible: New International Version.
Copyright © 1973, 1978, 1984 by the International Bible Society. Used by permission of
Zondervan Bible Publishers.

Text from When We Gather: Year B on pages 59-60 and 64-65 by James G. Kirk is used by
permission of Westminster /John Knox Press.

Selected lines from the poem "Savior" on p. 24 are from I Shall Not Be Moved by Maya Angelou.
Copyright © 1990 by Maya Angelou. Reprinted by permission of Random House Inc.

The excerpt on p. 131 is from "Calling All the Children Home." Words and music by John
McCutcheon © 1990 (Appalsongs/ASCAP). From the album "John McCutcheon. Live at Wolf
Trap" Rounder Records 0283.

The cover illustration titled "A Mother and Four Daughters" (detail), is from Sisters and
Prophets, Ave Maria Press, Notre Dame, Ind. © Mary Lou Sleevi, 1993.

96 97 98 99 00 01 02 03 04 05—10 9 8 7 6 5 4 3 2 1

MANUFACTURED IN THE UNITED STATES OF AMERICA

*With gratitude*

*To our mothers*

*June Little Childers and Anne Thompson Rose*

*And to the "mothers of homiletics"*

*Edwina Hunter and Joan Delaplane*

# Contents

# Introduction

A recent burst of national interest in gender communication has caused some segments of the church to haul out the old questions about women preachers. Stuck in a drawer for the last few years, they languished, waiting for insight to grow. "Is women's preaching different from men's preaching?" "In what ways?" "Why might it be different?" "Do women contribute anything to the discipline of preaching?"

In the church and in the academy, we have got as far as agreeing on a few general observations. Those of us who teach women preachers have compared our experiences and identified a few trends. (See Edwina Hunter's essay in *And Blessed Is She,* ed. David Farmer [San Francisco: HarperSanFrancisco, 1990], and Christine Smith's *Weaving the Sermon* [Louisville: Westminster/John Knox, 1989].) We believe, for example, that women's preaching makes somewhat greater use of story, especially story that is based on personal experience; that many women preachers hold a more communal view of authority than men tend to hold; and that the content of women's preaching may be shown to focus on justice themes more often than that of their male counterparts.

However, those of us who study preaching were still many carefully controlled studies away from being able to say much more than these kinds of things—or even to say these kinds of things without adding several qualifiers to the statements—when people in the pew, around the watercooler, and in the classroom's back row began explaining gender communication to one another.

"Women use 'rapport talk' and men use 'report talk,' " said one person who had stayed up the previous night reading *You Just Don't Understand* (Deborah Tannen, New York: Ballantine Books, 1990). "Men expend effort to avoid the one-down position in conversation while women expend effort to avoid the appearance of making a power play," said someone else who had just picked up Tannen's new volume, *Talking Nine to Five* (New York: William Morrow, 1994).

"Well, women have a way of undercutting their own credibility every time they open their mouths," said another who remembered hearing Robin Lakoff lecture on women's use of language. "Yes, and research shows that women preachers go out of their way to underplay their authority in the pulpit," said someone with a secondhand report of a small study by sociolinguist Frances Lee Smith. "If you ask me," the last person said, "I like women preachers. The one at my church is lively and interesting. What everyone has said about women may be true in the home and workplace, but in the pulpit they don't seem that different to me."

The questions about women preachers are out of the drawer and running around on the tabletops again. Are women preachers different from men preachers? Yes. Probably. In some ways. Spurred on by popular interest and the increasing numbers of women who are available to be studied, homileticians press on toward saying more. Despite the contribution of Deborah Tannen and others to this interesting discussion, it is still not possible to say with scientific certainty precisely how the preaching of women differs from that of men. But ask us if women enjoy sharing their resources with other women preachers (and with other interested preachers) and the answer is unambiguous, unqualified, and joyous, "Yes. Oh my, yes." That seems reason enough for this volume.

*Jana Childers*
*Lent 1995*
*San Anselmo, California*

# First Sunday of Advent

## *Marsha Foster Boyd*

**Isaiah 64:1-9:** This psalmlike poem voices the community's lament. The lectionary text represents most of the second half of the poem, an appeal for assistance.

**Psalm 80:1-7, 17-19:** This is a prayer for the restoration of Israel: "Let your face shine, that we may be saved."

**I Corinthians 1:3-9:** These verses follow Paul's opening greeting and express his thanks for the faith of the Corinthian church.

**Mark 13:24-37:** This apocalyptic-prophetic text describes the signs of the end and the tribulation. Since the timing is unknowable, the reader is exhorted to "Watch!"

## REFLECTIONS

I can't tell you how these lectionary passages troubled me as I kept trying to sit down to write this sermon. I can't tell you how many times I sat down, got up, sat down, and got up again, unable to reconcile these words with the joy that comes with knowing that Jesus is about to be born. After all, why would the writers have us read and reflect on such sad, gloomy, depressing words as these laments, at the beginning of the Advent season? I just couldn't figure it out.

Hear the people of Israel in Isaiah 64:1-9, God's people crying out in the exile to a God who would not answer:

O that you would tear open the heavens and come down, so that the mountains would quake at your presence— . . .

No eye has seen any God besides you, who works for those who wait for him. . . . But you were angry, and we sinned; because you hid yourself we transgressed. We have all become like one who is unclean, and all our righteous deeds are like a filthy cloth. . . . Yet, O LORD, you are our Father; we are the clay, and you are our potter; we are all the work of your hand. Do not be exceedingly angry, O LORD, and do not remember iniquity forever. Now consider, we are all your people.

And again, just listen to the people of Israel lifting their collective prayer in Psalm 80:1-6, another "group lament," to their God for deliverance:

Give ear, O Shepherd of Israel, you who lead Joseph like a flock! . . . Stir up your might, and come to save us! . . . How long will you be angry with your people's prayers? You have fed them with the bread of tears, and given them tears to drink in full measure. You make us the scorn of our neighbors; our enemies laugh among themselves.

Hear the refrain, repeated three times in this psalm: "Restore us, O God; let your face shine, that we may be saved." These lectionary texts trouble me.

# A SERMON BRIEF

These Old Testament passages tell us of a people who seem unable to hold out any longer, a people who have been waiting for God for a very long time, a God who is silent. And in Psalm 80, the people go so far as to remind God of God's great power and might exemplified in times past.

As I think about this waiting, this silence, I am reminded that in the African-American church tradition we sang: "I cried and I cried, I cried all night long. . . . My soul couldn't rest contented until I found the Lord." And the African-American poet Nikki Giovanni wrote some time ago: "All I ever do is sit and wait. . . ".

So, I was confronted with myself. Wanting Christmas—the joy, the fulfillment of the promise—but not remembering or wanting to acknowledge that in order to get there, one has to go *through* something, through the silence, through the darkness, through the anticipation of *waiting*.

One image that is used during this season of Advent is that of pregnancy; after all, we as women identify with Mary, "great with child," our pregnant sister. One often hears preaching women and men talk about the stress of going through a pregnancy, waiting, hoping for a happy, healthy baby, but waiting, not knowing whether all is well until the actual birth. It's an active waiting, waiting with anticipation.

But for some of us, this image brings up a different type of waiting: pain in the face of the silence of God, science, or circumstance. There are those of us who know another kind of waiting when it comes to babies—waiting to become pregnant and never becoming pregnant. What pain we sometimes feel, remembering. Remembering the anticipation month after month, year after year—waiting. Yes, you have to go *through* something. As preaching mothers who have given birth recount their trials as they waited, we recall different trials as we wait: "Restore us, O God; let your face shine, that we may be saved." *Where is this silent God?*

Now I see why I hesitated with these passages, why it was hard to encounter the "waiting moment." Some of those "moments" have been quite difficult and I wanted to hurry to the good news. All we have to do is watch television, listen to the radio, or read a newspaper and we know that "the whole world groans in travail until now."

The weather doesn't help; this is the time of year when the nights are long and the days are short. The *Diagnostic & Statistical Manual* has developed a term for a new psychological disorder that has emerged for those trying to cope with these seasonal changes: "seasonal affective disorder" (SAD). People are just trying to hold on, trying to hold out in the darkness, until the light comes.

I hoped that when I read the Gospel lesson for today, things would be different, I would get the good news I had been waiting for. The Gospel writer seemed to echo the anticipation of the Old Testament lessons, but this time the anticipation is for the coming Judgment of Christ. So this time it is the collective waiting of a bride (the church) adorned for her husband (the Christ). Some of us can indeed remember the anticipation of a bride, while others are still waiting!

This collective waiting also causes us, particularly women and men of color, to reflect on the situation of our people—locally, nationally, and globally. This period of history in which we live is also a period of collective anticipation of a mighty change, a cosmic upheaval that will bring new realities for everyone in the twenty-first century.

So, yes, we wait. We wait for the coming of Jesus in this time, this "not yet" time. We wait, knowing that he will come, he will enter our lives anew. But in the meantime, this in-between time of Advent, how will we determine to spend these waiting moments? What will we do for ourselves, for one another, for our God, in the meantime?

# Suggestions for Worship

## Call to Worship

Grace to you and peace, from God our creator and the Lord Jesus Christ. I give thanks to God always for you because of the grace of God that was given you in Christ Jesus. For in Christ, you have been enriched in every way. (I Cor. 1:3-9, adapted)

## Prayer of Confession

Oh, that you would rend the heavens and come down to us, O God. Oh, that the mountains would tremble before you. For we tremble in your presence, Mighty God. All of us have become like one who is unclean and our righteous acts are like dirty rags. We shrivel up like a leaf and like the wind our sins sweep us away. Yet, O God, you are our Maker. We are the clay, you are the potter; we are the work of your hand. Do not be angry beyond measure. Do not remember our sins forever. Look upon us we pray, for we are your people. Come down to us in mercy. (Isaiah 64, adapted)

## Assurance of Pardon (Isa. 65:17 adapted)

"For behold, I create a new heaven and a new earth," says our God. "And the former things shall be remembered no more."

## Benediction

The One who has called you is faithful
and will keep you strong to the end,
so that you will be blameless on the day
of our Lord Jesus Christ. (I Cor. 1:8-9, adapted)

The blessing of Israel's Shepherd be upon you.
The grace of the Risen Christ attend your way.
The power of the Holy Spirit reside within you—
And give you peace.

........................................................................

# Second Sunday of Advent

## Elizabeth Nordquist

........................................................................

**Isaiah 40:1-11:** The prologue of Second Isaiah announces good news in the poetic language that has become familiar: "Comfort, O comfort my people."

**Psalm 85:1-2, 8-13:** This prayer for peace affirms God's faithfulness. "Righteousness and peace will kiss."

**II Peter 3:8-15a:** The day of the Lord will come like a thief and heaven and earth will be dissolved. Meanwhile, those who wait for a new heaven and earth must be zealous to be found without spot or blemish.

**Mark 1:1-8:** The Gospel opens with the introduction of John the Baptist, "the voice of one crying out in the wilderness."

## REFLECTIONS

Two concepts in the II Peter passage need particular care and thought in terms of the sermon. First, although this text is assigned in the lectionary to the Advent cycle that we associate with Christ's birth, the focus of the writer is on the future "day of the Lord." Contemporary congregations have little information or few well-defined concepts about what this "day of the Lord" might entail. It is important to know what one's congregation believes or expects when such a text is read and preached. In some settings it is important to explain the concept of a "day of the Lord," beginning in the Prophets of the Old Testament, through Jesus, and places in the New Testament.

Second, the concept of the difference between the Greek words *chronos* and *kairos* can be very helpful and liberating. In contemporary culture, there is very little that honors anything but *chronos*. The concept that God has a different rhythm and schedule is one that can give great hope.

The four texts all focus on anticipation. The Isaiah 40 text may be the most familiar, and the most inviting; therefore, I used it as the call to worship. The Gospel lesson in Mark 1 picks up and reiterates that text, making it more specifically an announcement of the arrival of the Messiah, Jesus Christ. Psalm 85 gives voice to the frustration and confusion of waiting for God to become evident again, along with a beautiful affirmation of the reign of God when it appears, in verses 8-12. A beautiful setting of that text is found in the story "Babette's Feast" by Isak Dineson and in the movie made from the story.

# A Sermon Brief

Some of life's best experiences, best creations, and best hopes take time: a holiday fruitcake takes weeks to develop flavor; a spring garden is planted in the middle of autumn, months before there are any blossoms; a child takes years to become the person that God created her to be. Sometimes the waiting is hard. Advent honors the waiting that is required of us. In our journeys of faith, we not only allow for waiting, we value it; we wait for Christ to be born in us, and for Christ to return to us again.

The first hearers of the words of our text (II Pet. 3:8-15*a*) had been waiting for a long time—for Jesus to return to bring everything together, to bring perfect justice, to bring God's intended rule to heaven and earth. But time was dragging, there was no appearance of Jesus, and they were vulnerable to the ridicule of others and their own doubts.

The Epistle writer speaks the word of the Lord to the impatience and frustration that are beginning to characterize their waiting. The first word is that God's sense of time is not our sense of time. Humans have created clocks, calendars, datebooks, and timers—measurable, calculable time. Chronos kind of time. God operates on *kairos* time—holy moments, moments of fulfillment, moments of truth, moments of "Aha!" "With the Lord one day is like a thousand years, and a thousand years are like one day" (v. 8). God is operating on an entirely different system; therefore, God is not slow about the promise of Christ to return, as some people calculate slowness.

Beyond the different calculation of time, however, the Epistle writer says that God has a different understanding of "the day of the Lord" for which many of them long. The day of the Lord, the writer says, may not be an easy transition; there may be a great deal of noise, dissolution by fire, upheaval, fragmentation, pain and disorientation, in order for the new heaven and the new earth to be put in place. "You want Jesus to return, early Christians, but are you aware of the implications of becoming new, of being developed in your spirit to accommodate the new thing that God intends for humanity?"

We long for many things, but often are afraid of the process that we must go through to get them. We have visions, ambitions, dreams—for the immediate, for the future: a change in systems of power; a change in our own capacity to care; an increase in our physical strength and health; or restoration of peace on earth. In Advent we acknowledge that part of the process of change is waiting, and that part of the waiting is uncomfortable because it feels long, and makes us uneasy.

Women who bear children can concretely experience this ambiguity of waiting. Whether or not a woman was planning for the conception and birth of a child, a significant part of the nine month process is about waiting, and paying attention. There are new movements, contours, and sensations in her body and spirit that are ever-present reminders that new life is being formed in her, through her. Yet, she can do nothing about it; she can do everything possible to create a healthy space for the child within her and out in her environment. However, she cannot design the child; she cannot speed up the process. The child will be born in the *kairos* moment. And she must wait. In waiting she attends to her own health, her own spirit, her own wholeness watchfully and peacefully, until that moment comes.

I am aware as each Advent comes that the God whom we worship has plans for our good as humans, which are gestating, brewing, and simmering. Moreover, as each calendar year ends, beyond all the "ain't it awful" lists, there is evidence that God's healing is taking place, that words of peace are being spoken. Highways for our God are being formed, letting us know that the home of God, now and ultimately, is with women and men. On the other hand, each year I become more deeply aware that my activism, committees-without-end, and management-by-objectives will not bring an end to pain and fragmentation in me, the church, or in the world. Some things—the intended rule of God on earth—take time. And I, along with you, must wait.

How do we wait? Those early Christians were told to do two things: to be zealous to be holy (or whole), and to be at peace. In II Peter chapter one, the readers are exhorted to make every effort to supplement faith with virtue, virtue with knowledge, knowledge with self-control, self-control with steadfastness, steadfastness with godliness, godliness with friendly, family affection, and affection with love (II Pet. 1:5-7). This is holiness, or wholeness—integrity. To move toward holiness we must examine our motivations and behaviors, allow ourselves to ask the hard questions: Am I a woman of self-control? Am I a person who is faithful? Are we a godly group of people? Are we increasing in our repertoire of loving behaviors toward one another and the world? If not, Advent can be the opportunity for allowing the cleansing of the Spirit to blow through me, catch my attention, and purify me, so that there will be room for the Christ to be born, again, in me.

And then, says the writer, throughout this process be at peace. Holy waiting does not happen in frenzied activity, frantic racing around, or packed schedules. We are to be at peace, allowing the Spirit of God to replenish us with God's grace. A tall order for the week before Christmas, some of us might say. But how ironic it would be if we were to enter into the celebration of "Peace on Earth" with spirits that were frayed and ragged and unfocused because our waiting and anticipation were so frantic!

After a surgery, in which we know the results are good, comes the convalescence, where we monitor our progress each day, pay attention to the body, be awake to nourishment and movement, but peacefully wait, in comfort, for the body to heal itself. That is the way we are to spend Advent: staying alert to the movement of the Spirit, cooperating with its nourishment and cleansing, and then resting in peace, knowing that it is God who is at work in us both to will and to do God's good favor. Be holy and be at peace!

## SUGGESTIONS FOR WORSHIP

### Call to Worship (Isa. 40:1-5)

LEADER:   Comfort, O comfort my people, says your God.

PEOPLE:   Speak tenderly to Jerusalem, and cry to her that she has served her term, that her penalty is paid, that she has received from the LORD's hand double for all her sins.

LEADER:   A voice cries out:

PEOPLE:   "In the wilderness prepare the way of the LORD; make straight in the desert a highway for our God. Every valley shall be lifted up, and every mountain and hill be made low; the uneven ground shall beome level, and the rough places a plain.

ALL:   "Then the glory of the LORD shall be revealed, and all people shall see it together, for the mouth of the LORD has spoken."

### Prayer of Confession (in unison)

God of our salvation, we confess that we resent waiting, even for you. We are so accustomed to moving, thinking, caring, and acting quickly, that your sense of timing can make us feel frustrated and anxious. We also confess that we do not like some of the things that happen while we wait. We are appalled at continual violence, at widespread indifference to the needs and plights of the poor, weak, and disabled. We also know and confess that our very speed and impatience make us violent and uncompassionate also. We ask for your forgiveness, and we ask for the power of your Spirit to make us whole, holy people who reflect your image. We ask, too, that you create peace in us, as we learn to wait with open eyes to your presence in us and in the world. In the name of Jesus Christ whose coming we await. Amen.

## Assurance of Pardon (from Ps. 85:2-7 adapted)

LEADER:    The psalmist says:

> You forgave the iniquity of your people;
>     you pardoned all their sin.
> You withdrew all your wrath;
>     you turned from your hot anger.
> Restore us again, O God of our salvation, . . .
> Show us your steadfast love, O LORD.
> People of God, your sins are forgiven!

PEOPLE:    Thanks be to God!

## Benediction

May the God whose grace goes continually before us to save us, and Jesus Christ, who came to us and will come again, and the Holy Spirit who lives in us now to make us holy and bring us peace be our conscious companions as we continue to wait for the day of the Lord.

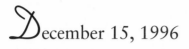
December 15, 1996

# Third Sunday of Advent

## Marsha Foster Boyd

**Isaiah 61:1-4, 8-11:** The voices of the prophet, Yahweh, and Zion blend in this poem that Jesus reinterpreted in the synagogue in Nazareth (Luke 4).

**Luke 1:47-55,** The Magnificat, or Psalm 126, Song of the Returning Exiles.

**I Thessalonians 5:16-24:** The benediction and closing of the letter: "Rejoice always . . . give thanks in all circumstances . . . hold fast to what is good."

**John 1:6-8, 19-28:** The testimony of John the Baptist. The priests and Levites are sent by the Pharisees to question John. He points to "the one who comes after me, the thongs of whose sandals I am not worthy to untie" (NIV).

## REFLECTIONS

"The Lord has done great things!" echoes—nearly verbatim—through these passages. Psalm 126:2, 3 and Luke 1:49 translate into those actual words. Isaiah 61 and Luke 1 chime in with litanies celebrating specific examples of what God has achieved. These powerful, sweeping texts do not stop at describing God's accomplishments. They add to the great things theme the idea that some of God's achievements have come about through *human agents*—women and men who have responded to the divine call.

John 1 reemphasizes the idea that human beings have a role to play in God's redemptive plan. And I Thess. 5:24 affirms this assertion, in case there are any still doubting God's ability to work through mere mortals with, "The one who calls you is faithful and he will do it" (NIV). Taken together, the lectionary texts for the third Sunday of Advent have less to do with the traditional "watch and wait" message, and more to do with a "get up and get ready" call.

Whether the intended audience is ready to hear God's word as it comes through the chosen messenger is always a question, as the text in John shows. Women preachers hardly need the reminder. There are still many "intended audiences" that resist women's preaching.

Elaine Lawless examines one segment of this resistance in her study of Pentecostal women preachers, *Handmaidens of the Lord* (Philadelphia: University of Pennsylvania Press, 1988). She concludes that it is precisely the strong sense of call that makes it possible for a woman to take to the pulpit in the face of opposition. Women "re-script" their lives, she finds. The women in her study are described as walking a fine line between the exercise of power and the acceptance of a subservient role, in order to accommodate their divine commission.

> Sometimes I'm called to a church and I run into a hard spirit at first. I say, "Relax, I don't call myself a preacher. Let the men do that; it's all right. But you have got to give me the right to be a handmaiden of the Lord and he has poured out his spirit unto me and he has called me into his work and I'm here." (Mary Harris, quoted in Lawless, 154)

> Hasten the day, O God—
> May the fine line walked by the
> Messengers who would prepare your way
> Open to a broad path.
> And may you—may you—
> come thundering down it.

## A SERMON BRIEF

What a blessing, what a blessing—to know that God's anointing falls on us, no matter who we are, when we are open to God's will in our lives; when we are open to being used by God for God's often mysterious and un-searchable purposes! This third Sunday of Advent plunges us deep into this reality, this reality of the anointing of God and our response.

In the Isaiah passage we read the call of the prophet, the affirmation of God's anointing on the prophet's life that equips the prophet for God's work. "The spirit of the Lord GOD is upon me, because the LORD has anointed me; he has sent me to . . . ."

This passage lets us know that God's anointing on our lives doesn't just come because God loves us, but because God desires to use us for a specific time and purpose. We are anointed to *do* something, to act!

In verses 1-3 we learn that this prophet was called and anointed to minister to God's people: to bring good news; to proclaim liberty, release, and the year of the Lord's favor; and to provide for those who mourn. In short, this prophet was anointed to minister to an oppressed people in particular ways.

Dr. Isaac R. Clark, my homiletics professor at the Interdenominational Theological Seminary, was an unforgettable man with an unforgettable teaching style. One of the many things he taught his students was that "God never makes any general calls." God calls each of us for a particular task. Dr. Clark used to admonish us that we should know exactly what we were called to do, and that if we didn't, then instead of moving ahead we needed to stay where we were until we heard God's specific instructions.

Now, you can imagine that for a group of young, energetic, reasonably intelligent, self-assured, would-be preachers, this admonition didn't sit too well! We didn't need Dr. Clark instructing us as to how to answer God's call! But, I'm also sure you know that eventually we learned the wisdom of Dr. Clark's words. Essentially, he was telling us that we needed to be sure—wait for God's anointing on our lives and our ministries to confirm the call and to empower us to do what it was that God was calling us to do—whatever that was. (For certainly that sainted man had heard enough of our bad sermons to know that preaching surely *wasn't* the calling in some of our lives!)

This leads me to the second passage for today found in the first chapter of Luke, the song of liberation sung by Sister Mary! Immediately upon reading this passage a song came to mind from the African-American gospel music tradition by Myrna Summers that says, "God gave me a song that the angels cannot sing." The song extols the majesty and power of the singer's God who "holds the power of the world in God's hand." This is Sister Mary's song of celebration that "God has done great things for me!"

Singing has always been an integral part of my being. In fact, my mother says that she had an angelic voice and could have done professional work, but that when I was born her singing voice left her and was passed on to me. I love to sing! So as I read this passage I could actually *hear* Sister Mary singing this song of freedom, vindication, and praise to her God.

The Reverend Dr. Gail Kennebrew Poindexter, supervisor of chaplains at a Chicago hospital, writes about the song of African-American women in her article "Releasing the Womanist Song" in *Womanist Care: How to Tend the*

*Souls of Women* (Chicago: Woman to Woman Ministries, Inc., 1991). The Reverend Poindexter asserts that the song of African-American women has been silenced by oppression from within and without. She says that the critical inner voices are silenced and healing takes place through women helping women—the song can and must be heard again!

Isn't that what happened between Elizabeth and Mary? It wasn't until they met following the Annunciation when Mary "went with haste" to Elizabeth's house that they both realized the fullness of the blessing of God on their lives. Indeed, when Mary greeted Elizabeth, not only did the baby in Elizabeth's womb "leap," but also the anointing fell on Elizabeth and she was "filled with the Holy Spirit." The whole atmosphere was charged with God's anointing power. Elizabeth confirmed the message of the angel to Mary, and I can imagine that they shouted over the truth that had been spoken to Mary concerning Sister Elizabeth: "with God nothing will be impossible." These women needed each other in order to gain the strength and courage to do what had to be done. What a wonderful model for ministry—to know that we are there to support and encourage one another as women! The confirmation and the anointing necessary to do the work came in community. Praise God!

So, no wonder Mary sang! No wonder she felt free to exalt her God, her "Strong Deliverer"! She couldn't keep it to herself! When one is assured of God's calling on one's life and God's anointing on the work and the worker, one can praise God unashamedly. And the song, once held captive by convention, by insecurity, by oppression can be released. Oh, to be anointed by God for service! Yes, Sister Mary had a song that the angels could not sing. And we do, too. A song emerging from our cultures, our families, our life experiences, and our relationship with our God. Let us learn to set that song free like Sister Mary did, so that the call and the anointing on our lives can bless others and bless God.

## SUGGESTIONS FOR WORSHIP

### Call to Worship

LEADER:   When the Lord restored the fortunes of Zion

**PEOPLE:   We were like those who dream.**

LEADER:   Then our mouth was filled with laughter

**PEOPLE:   And our tongue with shouts of joy.**

LEADER:    Then they said among the nations,
           "The Lord has done great things for them."

PEOPLE:    **The Lord has done great things for us.**

ALL:       **We are glad.** (Ps. 126:1-3)

## Prayer of Confession

> Petulant priests, greedy
> centurions, and one million
> incensed gestures stand
> between your love and me.
> Your *agape* sacrifice
> is reduced to colored glass,
> vapid penance, and the
> tedium of ritual.
> Your footprints yet
> mark the crest of
> billowing seas but
> your joy
> fades upon the tablets
> of ordained prophets.
> Visit us again, Savior.

(Excerpted from Maya Angelou, "Savior," *I Shall Not Be Moved* [New York: Bantam, 1990], 30)

## Assurance of Pardon

> Those who go out weeping,
>     bearing the seed for sowing,
> shall come home with shouts of joy,
>     carrying their sheaves. (Ps. 126:6)
> Friends, believe the Good News.
> In Jesus Christ, we are forgiven!

## Benediction

God gave us a song that the angels cannot sing.
With God, nothing will be impossible!

# December 22, 1996

# Fourth Sunday of Advent

## Elizabeth Nordquist

**II Samuel 7:1-11, 16:** Through Nathan's vision, God responds to David's desire to build God a house.

**Luke 1:47-55:** The Magnificat, or Psalm 89:1-4, 19-26: The psalmist celebrates the promise of God made to David through Nathan (II Samuel 7).

**Romans 16:25-27:** The conclusion of the letter to the Romans is doxological: "Now to God who is able to strengthen you . . . to the only wise God, through Jesus Christ, to whom be the glory forever!"

**Luke 1:26-38:** The Annunciation.

## REFLECTIONS

This passage about Mary and Elizabeth is rich with possibilities for women preachers, but also poses some questions of discernment regarding its interpretation. I assert that Mary made a thoughtful and intentional choice to receive the opportunity that she was offered by God. This assertion is different from that of some feminist exegetes who see this story as a passage about rape, and stands in contrast to those who see Mary as the completely docile and unconscious disciple of God, doing anything that she was asked to do. Mary's fear and ambivalence at the announcement of the angel is clear; the process of making a choice seems to take time. However, it is important for the preacher to represent Mary as one who is given a choice, and one who makes that choice thoughtfully.

There are important themes to be explored in the relationship of support and solidarity between Mary and Elizabeth, and how they affirm each other's experience and see the Spirit at work in the other. The ability of Elizabeth to celebrate Mary's particular call is a powerful model of sisterhood, or friendship, in the family of God.

The Old Testament passage, II Samuel 7:1-11, 16, lays the background of the Davidic covenant for the birth of the Messiah. That prophecy and promise is tied in Luke 1, both to Joseph's ancestry and to the prophetic prayer of Zechariah for his son, John the Baptist. Because the opening lines of the Psalm are about singing and God's promise, I use them as a call to worship to foreshadow the song of Mary that is to come. The passage from Romans 16:25-27 is a sweeping summary of the context into which the story of Mary and Elizabeth is set, and therefore serves as a good benediction.

# A SERMON BRIEF

Mary could have said no—
no to the angel invading her space;
no to the affirmation of her person by God;
no to the conception;
no to the birth;
no to the ministry of bearing, nurturing, raising, supporting, and following her Son, Jesus.
We can say no—
no to the call of God to each of us to follow;
no to the affirmation of our gifts, skills, and ministries;
no to the church of Jesus Christ in this world;
no to the work;
no to the mystery, the sacrifice and delight of a faithful call;
But Mary said yes:
"let it be to me according to your word."
And today we can say "yes" as we come to the end of Advent and enter into the celebration of Christmastide.
We are about to celebrate a birthing this week:
the birth of a child;
the birth of a Savior;
the beginning of a new, mysterious, wonderful thing that God has done and is doing in and for the world.
What made it possible for Mary to say "yes"?
What makes it possible for us to say "yes" to this birthing?
Elizabeth long ago out of her own journey toward a surprise birthing, knew what it took to say "yes."

"Blessed is she that believed that there would be a fulfillment of what was spoken to her by the Lord."

What did Mary believe? She had no formal theological training or official synagogue membership. But she did believe; her statement, "let it be with me according to your word," is the statement of faith. First, she believed that God was with her, as the angel said: the God of her mothers and fathers, the God of Israel, the God whose faithfulness and steadfast love had never wavered.

That God had many faces with which Mary was familiar from her ancestors:

Sarah knew a laughter-bringing God;
Hagar was discovered in the wilderness by the God of Seeing;
Leah praised the God who heard her cry;
Miriam danced to a triumphant God;
Hannah prayed to the Holy One, the Rock;
Ruth claimed the God who returned Mara to her home and to her original name, Naomi;
The widow of Zarepheth knew a God who kept oil in the jar;
The Queen of Sheba recognized a God of delight and love.

This God of Mary is a God whose presence can be trusted, can be believed. Mary believes God, the self-defining, "I AM WHO I AM." And so can we.

Mary also believed in herself. Lest this sound terribly narcissistic or egotistical, or like some trendy New Ageism, I need to explain. I believe that Mary had to believe in and trust in God's evaluation of her. The angel said, "You have found favor with God."

One of the gifts we are given on our faith journey is the awareness that not only does God love and redeem us, but that same God has created us in the image of God. Subsequently, we learn that by the gift of the Holy Spirit, God gives us spiritual gifts in addition to our natural talents and skills. Therefore, in the main when God has work to do in the world, human beings are called and equipped to do that work. However, some of us have a hard time believing that God would ever, could ever, choose us to do something worthwhile, something of significance in the world.

We don't believe that the person we have been created to be is valuable, is lovable to God, or can do anything worthwhile. Sometimes that belief is compounded by our sense of failure and our sense of sin, of having been and done less than what God has created us to be and to do. For those of us in that place, the temptation to sin by being less than God called us to be is greater than that of being too arrogant or too aggressive. It is all too easy to say "no" to God's birthing, because we do not think that we are able to do it, or are not worth it. We have no evidence that there was some kind of competition that Mary won in order to receive the ministry of raising Jesus—no nationwide search—only the word of the angel stating her qualification: God believed in her and called her, so she believed and said "yes."

God believes in us and calls us, too.

Most important, Mary believes in the process of the Spirit within her, in which she will participate. The angel had said, "The Holy Spirit will come upon you . . . ; nothing will be impossible with God." Mary was beginning a ministry journey as a cocreator with the Spirit of God. She could not do this alone, only with the Spirit; and the Spirit could not do this alone, only with Mary. Together they would be bringing into being Someone holy, Someone merciful, Someone strong. Someone who reallocates the resources of rich and poor so they all have what they need. Someone who is faithful from generation to generation. Not only will Mary be blessed; the world will be blessed. Mary believed, without knowing the particulars, that there would be a fulfillment of what was spoken to her by God, that she would have a part in it. We can believe that, too!

We have thousands of years of perspective on the ministry of Mary. Some traditions of the church have, I believe, done her a disservice by inflating her to nonbiblical, superhuman proportions—to be sinless, to be conceived immaculately, to remain a virgin perpetually, to be assumed bodily into heaven. Our Reformed Protestant tradition, pointing us to scripture alone, gives us enough to admire in Mary, without those traditions: She did indeed bring Jesus to birth in less than wonderful conditions; cared for him as a child, along with Joseph; supported his own emerging self-awareness of being the Messiah, even when she didn't really understand; couldn't intervene in or prevent his suffering or his death, yet watched it, was present to it; she visited his burial place; and she remained part of his faithful ones after he ascended to heaven.

I do not see her ministry as an easy one at all; but she was right: all generations have called her blessed, because she risked believing.

This last Sunday of Advent we all are invited to take the risk of believing that we, like Mary, are called: that the Lord is with us; that we have found favor with God; that the Holy Spirit has come upon us. And that we will be blessed if we believe.

There may be part of us that, like the Mary of Grunewald's altarpiece, are turning away, saying "Not me, Lord!" Part of us may be like Mary's cousin, Elizabeth, who, also filled with the Holy Spirit, says, "Why has this happened to me?" Part of us may be as elated as Mary was when she began to sing, "My soul magnifies the Lord . . . "

This ambiguity is part of the Advent journey of waiting. Mary could not figure out how this was to happen, but she said "yes!" to the vision. She could not deal with it alone, so she found her friend to sustain her. She did not know the outcome, but she traveled with Joseph to Bethlehem when she was invited. This is what believing in this Advent time looks like: saying "yes" to whatever opportunity God offers for bringing life to someone; sharing our story of

God's grace with someone else who has also experienced grace; and being willing to go where we are led to follow the light of Christ.

We have only a few days left in Advent, but they can be days of blessing if we believe: not in a formalized doctrine about God, but that our compassionate God cares about the quality and essence of our loving; not in our own natural organization and efficiency, but in the delight God has in who we are; not in the production that is Christmas, but in the Spirit of God that can infuse all our rituals and celebrations with holy hilarity.

We are blessed because we are loved by God, called by God, energized by God. Blessed are we if we believe that! Amen.

## SUGGESTIONS FOR WORSHIP

### Call to Worship (Ps. 89:1-2)

I will sing of your steadfast love, O LORD, forever;
  with my mouth, I will proclaim your faithfulness to all generations.
I declare that your steadfast love is established forever;
  your faithfulness is as firm as the heavens.

### Prayer of Confession (in unison)

Faithful, loving, and generous God, we confess that in the midst of all the holiday decorations, we are tempted not to believe—not to believe that you exist or care; not to believe that we are valuable to you and to others; not to believe that your Spirit is doing something new in and around us.

Forgive us, and lighten our hearts.

Help us see where you appear; help us listen to your voice; give us energy and will to go where you lead us this Advent time. In the name of the Christ child. Amen.

### Assurance of Pardon

The angel said to Mary, "Nothing will be impossible with God." Advent travelers, your sins are forgiven; your hopes will be realized; Christ is to be born! Amen!

### Benediction

After reading Romans 16:25-27, say, "Blessed are you who believe that there will be a fulfillment of what is spoken to you by the Lord!"

# Christmas Eve

## *Lynda Hyland Burris*

**Isaiah 9:2-7:** The prophet foretells the birth of a child, a sign that God will deliver the people from bondage.

**Psalm 96:** "Sing to the LORD a new song." This is a psalm of hope and promise that God reigns, despite the daily realities of evil, injustice, and brokenness.

**Titus 2:11-14:** In Christ, Paul says, "the grace of God has appeared."

**Luke 2:1-20:** This is the beloved story of the birth of Jesus.

## REFLECTIONS

Christmas Eve services often bring out the "once-a-year" Christians, drawn to the music, candlelight, and "magic" of the season. Many bring their children, and the preacher must be prepared to be inclusive and attentive to their hearing of the Story. In fact, one year a child asked me, "Do we have to hear that same story again?" In studying the text this year, I was struck by the image in Luke 2:7: "there was no place for them in the inn," which is often translated as "no room." One commentary on this passage suggests that it wasn't necessarily a fact that the inn was overcrowded that night, but that Joseph and Mary were not of the ilk who would "fit in." (Raymond Brown, *The Birth of the Messiah* [Garden City, N.Y.: Doubleday, 1979]: 399). Polly Berends's idea of "inn consciousness" versus "stable consciousness" seemed an appropriate introduction in considering how much room we give Jesus in our lives today: just on Christmas Eve, or year round? In the story portion of the sermon as well as the introduction, I have tried to be true to the historical context; to speak of our status as "inn people" or "stable people," while identifying those same differences in the biblical characters. Seeking a fresh perspective in presenting the text, I chose to tell the story from a woman's point of view, as well as use imagery that is feminine. It ends with an "altar call," or at least the hope that the hearer might look beyond the magical evening to a deeper relationship with Jesus Christ.

# A SERMON BRIEF

My friend Dorothy wrote a note in this year's Christmas card: "Yesterday I constructed a plastic box to cover two citrus trees in our backyard. This morning we saw a little brown bird inside, keeping warm while flitting about. My limited attention had been expanded—a box for a tree had become home to a little brown bird. Somewhere in this there lies an eternal message—a manger filled with straw received our Lord. God takes our limited visions and goals and works shining miracles of incarnation!"

While visions of sugarplums may still dance in some of our heads, we gather here, not seeking the magic of Mr. Claus, but yearning, hoping that something new and breathtaking will happen here. To us. In us.

In her book, *Gently Lead* (San Francisco: HarperSanFrancisco, 1992, 45-46), Polly Berends writes, "I think part of the appeal of the Christmas story and why we love babies in general so much is that we yearn to be pure and innocent and clean, good again to have a fresh start and be truly lovable and loving.

"So it's good to consider what the conditions were under which the Christ Child got born. Suppose the inn and the stable are really just two states of mind. What is the Inn Consciousness in which there is 'no room' for the Christ Child? What is the inn too full of? People. Inn Consciousness is a headful of people trying to get ahead, looking out for themselves, by wheeling and dealing, prostituting, influencing, jockeying for position, and trying to get comfortable at each other's expense. It is very crowded and un-stable. Here there are only strategies, and it is no place for the Christ Child to be born.

"What about the stable? In the stable are only lowly animals—beasts of burden. They don't think they know what's good for them. They don't have much and they aren't trying to get more. They don't worry about the future or where the next meal is coming from. They trust, serve, and are interested to see what's next. They are humble, open, and willing, like a baby. That's where the Christ Child gets born. All you have to do to maintain a stable is to keep shoveling out the manure and bringing in fresh food. To maintain Stable Consciousness all you have to do is keep shoveling out the 'should,' keep letting in fresh inspiration and be willing to do what is called for. That's where the Christ Child gets born." Prepare him room. In the crude stables of our hearts, he is born. In real life we sometimes find ourselves over at the inn; sometimes, back at the stable. Listen, again, to the story of one from the inn, who went to the stable.

Once upon a time . . . for isn't that the way all life's stories are to begin? Yet I remember it as though it were this very night. Oh, I wish you could have been there!

Ah, it was such a night—a magical, mystical, awesome night—a holy night. A night that changed my life forever. No one much remembered my part in it, but that's all right. What people do recall is how my husband, God rest his soul, shut the door on them. But he had a lot on his mind: keeping the accounts in order, feeding the animals, putting food on the table, changing the bedding. You know . . . all the details, all the things that it takes to run a business.

Well, maybe he was a bit brusque with them, a little sharp. But he really meant no harm. And you have to understand, the inn was packed to the rafters that night. There really wasn't any room. All these folks had crowded into town for the census. Of course, those who had family or friends living here stayed with them. And these two, this couple, well, they just weren't our kind; you could just tell. It was something about them—their clothes and their ways were different from ours.

But I digress. I'll never forget the moment they walked through the door. Sam—that's my husband—was going over the books, and I was sitting there too, by the light of the lamp, mending a piece of cloth.

I looked up and there they were. She moved as though she were walking on sand, slowed by the fullness of her blossoming belly. It wouldn't be long now, I thought. I held my breath at the sight of her. The man—I knew he wasn't her husband—was real soft, gentle-spirited, not belligerent and rowdy like some people get. And he looked—hungry.

All I remember at this point is how dark it was. When the door opened the sky behind them looked purple, not like the usual blackness of a winter night. I remember that, the color purple. And I felt as though I were waiting for something to happen. And then the lamp went out, and I blinked my eyes at the purple sky, and them silhouetted against it. Somehow, the lamp was lit again, and Sam seemed to hang his head and said, "No room." As they turned to go, her eyes met mine. She was so young, just a girl really, and her eyes were huge and dark with fear, and yet calm and deep at the same time.

"Wait," I whispered. "Wait. What about the stable, Sam?" I said. She never took her eyes off me, and they shone with gratitude, as Sam led the way around back of the inn.

The inn was noisy that night, almost festive, even though the occasion was nothing to celebrate. The census, I mean. Some folks started singing, and others joined in, and music filled the front room and warmed the air.

Then, as one song ended, a hush fell over the room. And in that stillness, a baby began to cry. Everyone stopped, almost frozen in place, and listened. Until some raspy-voiced old man said, "Make that kid quiet down."

I stood up, my mending dropped to the floor, and I said, "No. Don't shush the baby. We need to hear the baby. The baby is our music." I don't know what came over me, or why I said what I said. But soon the crowd resumed its own chattering. And the singers started to sing another tune. I wrapped my shawl tight around my head and face, and went out the door.

Oh, the night! So purple and dark! And the stars looked like flowers blooming, like white flowers blossoming all over the sky. And one, burning so bright, like the sky would break open, was hanging just over the stable there. So I followed, by its light, along the path around the back, to the stable. And there, by the light of that star, amidst the stinking breath of the oxen, lying in the straw, in the manger, I saw him. "What child is this?" I whispered. Her eyes met mine again. And she smiled the slow, sweet smile of a mother relieved of her labor. The man knelt down in the straw beside her, looking down with amazement at this swaddled bundle of baby. I don't know why, or how, but I stretched out my arms to him, to the baby. Me, motherless, barren, without any idea how to care for a child! I stretched out my arms to him. I felt like I'd waited so long—all my life, really—for this moment to come, and I stretched out my arms to him. And the mother said with her eyes, "Take him. Take the baby."

On this night, this holy, wondrous, silent night—will you? Will you prepare him room? Will you take him? Will you take the baby? Now?

## SUGGESTIONS FOR WORSHIP

### Call to Worship (based on Psalm 96)

LEADER:    Sing a new song to the Lord [God]!

**PEOPLE:**    **Sing to the Lord [God], all the earth!**

LEADER:    This night, God has given us a New Song to sing.

**PEOPLE:**    **So sing, earth and sky! Roar with your music, sea, and all creatures within you.**

LEADER:    Dance, fields and meadows; sing for joy, all the trees of the forest!

ALL:    **For God is coming! God comes tonight, singing a New Song of justice, truth, and love.**

## Prayer of Confession

O God of Light, we do not always see you or seek you in the darkness of our days. We feel the burdens of too much to do, too little time; too many people in pain, too few hands to help, and we are weighed down. We sit in the shadows, feeling sorry for ourselves and frightened for the world around us. Give us a sign, God; grant us peace.

## Assurance of Pardon

Hear the good news: A child has been born for us! And he is named Wonderful Counselor, Prince of Peace, Emmanuel, Jesus the Christ! I say to you, in his name, our darkness is gone, our sins are forgiven! Glory be to God in the highest. Amen.

## Benediction

Go forth, this silent, holy night
Bearing God's Christmas light.
May the miracle of Christ's birth,
The love of God's life on earth,
And the Spirit's flame and power
Fill you in this hour and always. Amen.

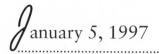

# Epiphany

## *Lynda Hyland Burris*

**Isaiah 60:1-6:** The prophet proclaims to Israel their radiant relationship to God. In Christian interpretation, the light is a christological symbol, and an analogy is made to the light of the star that the Magi followed.

**Ephesians 3:1-12:** Paul reveals how the mystery of Christ was offered to him through the grace of God.

**Matthew 2:1-12:** Herod and the Magi seek the Christ Child; the journey and visit of the Magi.

## REFLECTIONS

Recognizing that the popular trend is not to preach on the Epiphany event but to focus instead on alternate texts on the baptism of Jesus, I defy the trend and choose Matthew's powerful and dramatic story of the Magi's journey. Do we move away from this passage because of the three wise men? If so, we lose the opportunity to offer assurance to women and men of God's manifesting God's self throughout history, and in our world today. In studying Matthew's text as well as the Isaiah passage, the symbols of light (radiant, shine, star) are readily apparent, and are appropriate to emphasize as beacons of hope on a dark winter Sunday of the new year.

Including the folk tale of Befana (who is Babushka in the Russian version), I sought out a story that would retell the journey of the Magi and include a woman. She is, in fact, more realistically "human" than the wise ones themselves, and represents all our human resistances and blockades to letting God in our lives. The primary focus of the sermon is seeking—and it is hoped finding—God in our lives, with the idea that the church is one place where God may be revealed to us. The secondary focus is that we are given a choice—to seek the Christ and follow him; to seek him, find him, and choose to turn away; or, like old Befana, to be too busy, too late, or too self-absorbed to "see the light."

# A Sermon Brief

And when the star "stopped," so the story goes, they found him, amidst the sweet scent of hay and the sour stench of manure. In gentle glow, like a single candle lit in the dark black night, they found him.

We call this story, this event, Epiphany. The word "epiphany" comes from the Greek word meaning "manifestation." Epiphany is both a day, and a season of the church year. It is a celebration of Jesus manifesting God to the world. The Magi (the wise men) represent us, the whole human race, and Jesus is revealed as God to them (and to us), the light of the world.

We now know that the wise men were not kings, that they probably weren't riding camels and that they came sometime later than the birth of Jesus, probably when he was eighteen months to two years old. Matthew even tells that they came to a house, not a stable. What Matthew wants to emphasize is our relationship, through the Magi, to Jesus.

To many people this event, this Epiphany, is neither a familiar church celebration nor even a known word. And it's no wonder: it comes after Christmas, when we often feel tired of the festivities, and are ready to return to routine. It is the new year, and we are filled with new resolve to do whatever it was we didn't do last year. Christmas is past; it was last year. Now we have Super Bowl Sunday to look forward to!

It is a tradition in our home to host an Epiphany dinner each year. The menu features French American cuisine—chosen because the French celebrate Epiphany or Twelfth Night so enthusiastically.

The evening includes the serving of the Twelfth Night cake, a light and flaky bit of pastry, filled with hazelnuts and—one small figurine of the baby Jesus. Tradition dictates that the person who finds the baby figurine in his or her serving will have good fortune in the new year. The person is crowned king or queen of the night, and is expected to host next year's feast.

The first year my family began this custom, the dinner guests were a prominent group of theologians—a seminary professor, a seminary president, and a well-known author and preacher. As you might imagine, a fairly intellectual, heady bunch. When I explained the tradition of the Twelfth Night cake, telling a wonderful story about a woman I'd read about who had been crowned the Queen of Twelfth Night, there were snickers and cynical smiles around the table, except for one prominent guest, who exclaimed, "I want the baby Jesus! I want to get the baby Jesus!"

Many share that feeling. Columnist Anna Quindlen writes, "Each year around this time, thousands of Americans come to church, looking for something. For some it is simply a search for some shred of childhood ritual, a past form without present belief. For those holding the hands of their children, it is often a search for that thing that parents always want for their family, a direction in a world that seems without compass" ("Soul Searching," *Santa Rosa* (California) *Press Democrat*, 5 January 1991, B4).

Following that star, which may have dimmed over the years, they've come looking for the baby. Haven't we all? "Where is he?" is whispered in many hearts, in the darkness of our own doubts at one time or another.

Yes. Christmas is packed up and put away for another year. For some who come to see the baby, they can go home confident that he'll be here next year when they come back. Yet others may still breathe the words "Where is he?" into the cold night, even after candlelight and carols on Christmas Eve. Yet I would suggest that in each of our lives there are moments that might be named "epiphanies," those crystal clear experiences where God shines through another's eyes or the ambience of a room feels awash with the light of God's glory, while time seems to hang suspended in midair.

Such a moment came about one year when the youth group and I took a Christmas tree and handmade ornaments down to the family shelter. We brought cookies and small gifts and sang carols with the children and their parents. The lights were strung, and the decorations hung when Maria commented that we had no star for the top of the tree. A couple of minutes later she returned, offering a construction paper star, glistening with glitter, made by one of the shelter children. Maria made a paper cone and attached the star to it. Simple. Beautiful.

The lights were dimmed, except those on the tree, and we started to sing, all of us, home-less and home-full. Then one of the teenage girls picked three-year-old Leah, a child from the shelter, and I handed her the star. Leah was lifted up and she placed the star on top of the tree. "Silent night, holy night," we sang. "All is calm, all is bright." A tiny, homeless child, reaching up, holding the star. Epiphany.

Following the star to Bethlehem was not the end of the Magi's journey, nor is it ours. Bethlehem is just the beginning. Matthew tells us the wise men were overwhelmed with great joy, they bowed down and worshiped him, and they brought him gifts. And then they went back into the night, and continued their journey home. In his book, *Magnificent Defeat*, author Frederick Buechner suggests that the reason they left was that the Magi saw, or foresaw,

Jesus' death, that "it sat on his head like a crown" (68). And that to stay with him would be to share that death.

So some folks turn away after Christmas. Because the baby we welcome in the gentle, soft light of a Christmas Eve grows up—announcing hope for humanity, pushing the limits of all those in religious and social power. The Light of the World was a fierce, growing ember in life, a torch that flamed through the darkness, and burns still—in the epiphany moments of our lives.

Through God we have been given a chance—like Herod—to turn away from him in silent hostility, threatened by his power, his radiant light. Or to turn toward him, and like the Magi, bow down. Those wise ones may have seen the shadow of death surrounding him, but within him—they saw the light of life.

The sermon concludes with the story of Befana, and ends with the following:

But Old Befana never caught up to the three kings—she is searching still to this day, so the story goes. Every year on the Feast of Epiphany, Old Befana runs across the sky.

"Where is he?" she whispers.

And we answer, "He is here." Let us bow down and lay our gifts before him.

## SUGGESTIONS FOR WORSHIP

### Call to Worship

LEADER:    Arise, shine, for your light has come!

**PEOPLE:**    **The child has been born, the king of the Jews!**

LEADER:    The glory of the Lord has risen upon you!

**PEOPLE:**    **The Messiah has come!**

LEADER:    See and be radiant; thrill and rejoice.

**ALL:**    **We bring our gifts and proclaim the praise of God!**

### Prayer of Confession

In the darkness of winter's morn, we pull the covers over our heads, trying to block out your light of love, O God. We don't want to rise and shine, God, we want to sleep. Day after day, dazed and dulled by the despair of the world, we want to close our eyes. We look for you only when we need you, forgetting that you look out for us, and all our needs, all the time.

## Assurance of Pardon

Lift up your eyes and look around. A bright new day has dawned. God's light has come. God's light shines still. The light of the world burns still. Believe the good news: In Jesus Christ we are forgiven.

## Benediction

May the revelation of God's love, the light who is Jesus the Christ, and the radiance of the Holy Spirit dawn in you, fill you, and through you, be revealed to all the world. Amen.

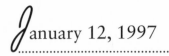

January 12, 1997

# Baptism of the Lord
# (Ordinary Time 1)

## *Linda L. Clader*

Genesis 1:1-5: The first day of creation.

Psalm 29: "The voice of the LORD is over the waters."

Acts 19:1-7: Paul prays for the disciples in Ephesus. They receive the Holy Spirit.

Mark 1:4-11: The appearance of John the Baptist, Jesus' baptism.

## REFLECTIONS

The following portion of a homily focused tightly on Mark's story of the baptism of Jesus, with its emphasis on the good news of God's forgiveness. (For a full and clear exposition of this understanding of the good news, see L. William Countryman, *Good News of Jesus: Reintroducing the Gospel.* [Boston: Cowley Publications, 1993.]) One might, however, draw from all four lections to preach both Baptism and Epiphany, using the action of God's Word as the key. Genesis presents "a wind from God . . . [sweeping] over the face of the waters" churning up the chaotic stuff of creation in the manner of a whirlwind or thunderstorm—a God much like the Lord being celebrated in Psalm 29. And yet creation happens not through an incomprehensible howl of wind or storm, but through God's speech, which brings order out of chaos by naming the first element into being. The God of Israel is thus a God whose creative power is manifested in the spoken Word.

The lessons from both Mark and Acts focus on the action of the Holy Spirit in the context of baptism; indeed, the very presence of the Spirit distinguishes the baptism of Jesus Christ from the baptism of John. But it is striking that in both stories the Spirit's movement is signaled by speech: a voice from heaven accompanies the appearance of the descending dove, naming Jesus as God's Son, and after the Spirit drives him into the wilderness, Jesus responds by beginning to proclaim the good news on his own (Mark 1:12-14). When the disciples receive the Holy Spirit at the hands of Paul, they begin to speak in tongues and to prophesy, and examples abound throughout the book of Acts where the immediate effect of the Spirit is the ability to speak, often before hostile audiences (e.g., 1:16; 2:4, 17-18; 4:8, 25, 31; 6:10; 10:44-46; 13:9-11; 19:6; 21:4, 11 [See R. C. Tannehill, *The Narrative Unity of Luke-Acts: A Literary Interpretation,* vol. 2 of *The Gospel According to Luke Series* (Philadelphia: Fortress Press, 1986), 233]).

In baptism, we are named as God's children, incorporated into the Body of Christ, and empowered by the Holy Spirit for ministry. Thus today we worship a God whose Word names us into being; we acknowledge the Word Incarnate into whose Body we are being grafted; and by the power of the Holy Spirit we proclaim the gift and the responsibility of being the bearers of the Word in the world.

## A SERMON BRIEF

What drew Jesus to the river that day,
    that day when John was baptizing, proclaiming a baptism of
    repentance?
    Did Jesus feel a need for repentance? Could he have seen
    himself as a sinner?
Or, maybe, did he feel a need to make an outward, visible
    sign of his total reliance on God—because that's what
    repentance is too, recognizing our utter dependence on
    God's love and care—was that why he was there?
The Gospel of Mark doesn't start with Jesus' genealogy, like
    Matthew's version; it doesn't start with dreams and visions
    and angels and shepherds, like Luke's version; and it
    doesn't start with theological hymns, like John's version.
The Gospel of Mark starts here, with the baptism of John,
    with Jesus coming to the river
    and undergoing a baptism of repentance for the forgiveness of
    sins.
Mark's story of Jesus *begins* with repentance.
    Mark's story of Jesus *begins* with forgiveness.

Jesus comes to John, to the water of baptism.

> We don't know what he was thinking; we don't know why he
> was there.

But he did what the others did.

> The others, who were there to confess their sins,
>> to make an outward and visible sign of their reliance on
>> God.

Jesus did that.

Jesus began his public life with a strong, public affirmation—

> that he, too, was dependent on God's forgiveness,
> that God's forgiveness is what it's all about!

And then—what happens?

Imagine what that must have been like.

> You've been praying. You've humbled yourself.
> You've confessed your utter dependence on God alone.
> You've taken John's hand,
>> and you've waded into the river and you've plunged under
>> the cool water,
>> and now you're regaining your feet, and your head breaks
>> the surface,
>> and the water pours down your shoulders, and you feel the
>> warmth of the sun on your face,
> and you hold out your hands to bask in it,
> and suddenly you see the heavens break apart,
> and you see and you feel the Spirit of God falling upon you,
> and you hear a voice—a voice speaking words
> that you've been hearing from the scriptures ever since you
> could speak—
> you hear a voice from heaven saying,
>> "You are my child, the beloved: with you I am well
>> pleased."

Imagine what that must have been like!

Imagine hearing that you are God's child, the beloved!

Imagine hearing that God is well pleased with you!

Imagine the feeling of elation—the feeling of empowerment!

> The Spirit of God is in me! I am God's child, God's chosen!
> What shall I do with all the energy I feel?
> What shall I do with all the courage I feel?
> I have to spread the news! Where shall I begin?

Imagine what that must have been like!

And it all began, Mark tells us,

> it all began with an outward and visible sign of total

reliance on God;
   it all began with a public declaration of faith in God's
   forgiveness.
Imagine what that must have been like!
But every one of us who has been baptized has, in fact, had this
experience.
Do we remember coming to the water of baptism,
   acknowledging our dependence on God,
      renouncing evil and asking for an outward and visible sign
         of God's forgiveness and our new life?
Do we remember the water pouring over our faces? Do we remember
   that rebirth?
Maybe we don't remember—but we did it.
Do we remember the heavens opening? Do we remember the Spirit
   descending upon us?
   Maybe we don't remember—but it happened.
Do we remember the voice, speaking the words of generations of
   prophets,
      linking our lives with the chosen ones of Israel;
      linking our lives with Jesus himself—
         with his life and his death and his resurrection?
Maybe we don't remember—but at our baptism, that voice did speak,
   naming us, too:
   "You are my child, my beloved. In you I am well pleased."
That's what we did, that's what we are doing in our baptism:
   We're participating in the life of Jesus Christ.
   We're dying to the life of fear, the life of defensiveness,
      the life of militant privateness.
   We're being reborn to the life of courage, the life of
      faithfulness,
      the life of transparency in the power of God.
And this new life, this empowered life
   is founded first and foremost on the knowledge of God's
   forgiveness.
*This* is the knowledge, the reality, the assurance
   that offers us the strength, the courage, and the faith
      to strive for justice, to be the hands and feet and voice
      of God in the world
      to offer to others the healing word of God's forgiveness.
*This* is the good news that Jesus proclaimed.
*This* is the declaration of new life.
*This* is the foundation of Christian hope.
*WE HAVE BEEN FORGIVEN!*

## Suggestions for Worship

This Sunday is traditionally designated as especially appropriate for the service of Holy Baptism. Whether or not there is to be a baptism, it is advisable to focus liturgically on that sacrament through a Renewal of Baptismal Vows by the congregation (e.g., *The Book of Common Prayer,* [New York: Seabury Press, 1979], 304).

## Call to Worship

LEADER:     Blessed be God: Father, Son, and Holy Spirit.

**PEOPLE:     And blessed be God's kingdom, now and forever.**

LEADER:     There is one Body and one Spirit;

**PEOPLE:     There is one hope in God's call to us;**

LEADER:     One Lord, one Faith, one Baptism;

**PEOPLE:     One God and Father of all** (based on *The Book of Common Prayer,* 299).

## Prayer of Confession

*(time for silent prayer of confession)*

Father in heaven, who at the baptism of Jesus in the River Jordan proclaimed him your beloved Son and anointed him with the Holy Spirit: Grant that all who are baptized into his Name may keep the covenant they have made, and boldly confess him as Lord and Savior; who with you and the Holy Spirit lives and reigns, one God, in glory everlasting. Amen (*The Book of Common Prayer,* 214).

## Benediction

May Almighty God, who led the Wise Men by the shining of a star to find the Christ, the Light from Light, lead you also, in your pilgrimage, to find the Lord. Amen.

May God, who sent the Holy Spirit to rest upon the Only-begotten at his baptism in the Jordan River, pour out that Spirit on you who have come to the waters of new birth. Amen.

May God, by the power that turned water into wine at the wedding feast at Cana, transform your lives and make glad your hearts. Amen.

May the blessing of God Almighty, the Father, the Son, and the Holy Spirit, be upon you and remain with you forever. Amen (*The Book of Occasional Services* [New York: 1979, 22]).

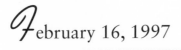

# First Sunday in Lent

### *Barbara Bate*

**Genesis 9:8-17:** God's covenant is established with Noah, his descendants, and every living creature: Never again shall there be a flood to destroy the earth. The rainbow is a sign of this promise.

**Psalm 25:1-10:** This psalm is a prayer of supplication: "Teach me your paths."

**I Peter 3:18-22:** This difficult text describes Christ preaching to those "who in former times did not obey, . . . in the days of Noah."

**Mark 1:9-15:** Jesus is baptized in the Jordan by John. The Spirit descends in the form of a dove. His forty days in the wilderness and return to Galilee are briefly described.

## REFLECTIONS

The four texts for this Sunday offer images of covenant, along with connections between God and the flesh. Covenant is essential in these texts, in the promise to Noah, in the baptism by John, and in the ultimate gift of Jesus to humankind. It is a continuing preoccupation in both the Hebrew Bible and the New Testament scriptures.

In preparing for this preaching event I wanted to find ways to help embody the divine-human experience of Jesus as a holy and holistic covenant. I have found that many women experience their life journeys as a cluster of relationships rather than a linear series of separate events. Yet the questions they are asked, whether filling out résumés or even meeting other adults for the first time, imply that one should be able to put experiences together in a finite, easy-to-follow form.

Commentaries on Mark often center on the messiahship of Jesus instead of the human that confronted the testing in the desert. It is easy to emphasize only the Word and forget that Jesus was also made flesh. I hope in the text to be faithful to a more accessible Christology, and to continue my own commitment to the empowering of women through stories.

# A SERMON BRIEF

It is a story of incredible compactness and variety. In barely 130 words in the New Revised Standard Version of the Gospel of Mark, Jesus virtually swoops into view. He is seen emerging from his hometown of Nazareth, comes out of the baptismal waters of the Jordan River, is called "beloved" by voice and dove, is tempted by Satan in the desert, and is brought into active ministry in Galilee. The journey reads like a brief spot announcement on television, telling a most incredible story from many angles.

Whenever I look at this passage I'm struck by the way Jesus' journey into ministry and trouble is so full and yet so sparse. It's not clear why all of this essential information was presented in such a brief form. Perhaps the story was already familiar to Mark's community. Perhaps the reports of Jesus' baptism, his honoring as the messiah, and his successful testing in the desert were less at issue for the evangelist than the impact of Jesus' ministry in Galilee and his gathering of the disciples. In any event it seems noteworthy that this whirlwind narrative at the start of Mark's Gospel gives us both blessing and struggle centered on Jesus.

While he is in the desert, Jesus is said to be found with the wild beasts and ministered to by angels. Though Mark's account of the temptation is more brief than those of Matthew and Luke, it includes, as they do, the mention of a lengthy "forty days" of testing. His authority is bracketed with his vulnerability. Accompanied by wild beasts, he cannot be considered more of a prophet than John the Baptist, whose imprisonment is also reported. Served [as in the term *diakonos*] by angels, he cannot be at the same time a leader in ministry. The mixture of items and images does not seem to be accidental. The grappling with the mixture of divinity and vulnerability is essential to the way the Jesus story emerges. It is also the way the stories of so many of us are woven together.

Many years ago I became acquainted with Susan, a woman who was highly regarded as a professor and a trainer of counselors. She recounted to me the life history of one of her students, a young woman who had gone through enough trauma to make almost anyone buckle—major illness, marriage failure, loss of a child, financial problems, and clinical depression. I commented in Susan's presence that I could not imagine someone with that many troubles being a therapist for other people. Her response surprised me. "I'm not worried about her. She's been through all these things and come out on the other side. She will not be shocked at the experiences of other people. She is likely to empathize better than a person who has tended to have an easy time in life." I realized after hearing her response that I had been imagining empathy as depending on the empathic person as "having it all together"—whatever that meant—rather than having the capacity to stand fully in another's presence.

Part of the mystery/intrigue in the characterization of Jesus, especially in Mark, is that we are given the chance, even forced, to absorb the story amid paradox and contradiction. There are major questions and gaps in the story, most obviously in the various possible endings for the Gospel itself. We are called repeatedly to make our own judgments about the words, meanings, and impact of an ambiguous messiah.

During much of the New Testament canon, and in much Christian preaching, the divinity of Christ has been illuminated so brightly that those in the pews could spend their lives never hearing that Jesus was both God and human. Without that conviction, however, we have no basis for finding an image of God within ourselves. The testing in the desert makes clear that Jesus was and is not a platitude but a person. Being surrounded by wild beasts and being supported by angels renders the prophet and healer able to know what it is to be deeply in need.

How do people learn to live into and live with their stories? In a sense this early narrative in Mark is a microcosm of what people go through when they meet a new person or a new situation. Telling your story demands making choices of emphasis and value. What seems "major" in my life thus far? What is guiding me in the direction I am going? How will other people hear me, and how will I hear myself? Theologian and educator Nelle Morton has used the phrase "hearing someone into speech" in her book *The Journey Is Home.* That phrase evokes the psychological and spiritual power that can emerge when telling one's own story in the presence of another. Many women have described the experience of going through incredible pain in their lives, and yet finding significant meaning and hope in sharing those experiences.

Mark's story is not exactly my story. But because it gathers up so quickly and so fully the God-story that I want to know and hear, it calls me to take up again the journey that the Christian community calls the season of Lent. The journey is a new one each year, sometimes apparently "better," sometimes not. Whatever the particulars of this season's narrative, there is always a pull toward a new reading of the possible. How will I hear and tell about the bracketed blessings and testings of my life, or of our lives? The journey goes on.

## SUGGESTIONS FOR WORSHIP

### Call to Worship (in unison)

In this journey,
A beginning, a vision, a blessing,
A prophet, a healer, a teacher,
The water, the voice, and the dove.
In this journey,
Our hope and our struggle for meaning,
Our turning again toward the future;
God's challenge to hear and believe.
In this journey,
As we look for a way in the desert,
As we listen for silence and stillness,
Keep us faithful, O God, in your presence.

### Prayer of Confession

The world is full of temptations, O God. Not just the obvious ones that we call power and envy and hatred and lust, but the subtle ones of despair and apathy, of giving in and giving up. It is possible to decide that we just don't matter enough to have the attention of the Holy One. After all, Jesus had the authority of God and the tools of preaching and teaching and healing. Many of us have not found any gifts worth mentioning in our own record of accomplishments in life.

Yet Jesus was tested in the wilderness. That gives us a glimpse of one who knew what it was to be lost and alone. Depression, confusion, and anger can also be wild beasts of the spirit. People who listen to us in loving friendship can be angels in disguise. So faith is not finally a matter of seeking perfection. It is growing toward covenant together, a glimpse of a journey we share.

### Assurance of Pardon

Before us is an everlasting covenant, between God and every living creature that is on the earth. Thanks be to God for this everlasting love. Amen.

## Benediction

May God be a blessing to you by the river;
May God keep you safe in the desert;
May God challenge and affirm you on the journey;
In the name of Jesus, Amen.

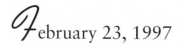

# Second Sunday in Lent

*Mary J. Scifres*

**Genesis 17:1-7, 15-16:** God promises Sarah a child.

**Psalm 22:23-31:** God rules over all nations and generations.

**Romans 4:13-25:** God's promise depends on faith.

**Mark 8:31-38:** "Take up [your] cross and follow me."

## Reflections

**Genesis 17,** the primary text for today's sermon, is part of the lengthy narrative describing God's covenant with Sarah and Abraham. This particular passage relates to the promise of a child to the barren Sarah. The longer story includes Genesis 11:29-30; 12:1-20; 15:1–18:15, 20; 21:1-20; and 22:1-19. Sarah's barrenness is no small matter, since her inability to bear a child threatens the very basis of God's promise to make Abraham and Sarah the ancestors of a great nation. Her story is the beginning of a series of barren matriarchs who will give birth to this nation in spite of great obstacles. When preaching any of these texts of barrenness, the preacher is wise to remember that many women and men in our congregations suffer silently as they deal with the pain of infertility or chosen childlessness that is not always accepted in church communities. Hope can be preached to these people when we help congregations to see ways to offer family to one another, to understand that the family of today (and yesterday) consists of many diverse relationships, and to realize that neither barrenness nor fertility is a commentary on God's approval or disapproval of our lives and our actions.

**Romans 4:13-25** is a text of faith, appropriate during the Lenten season. However, these words of Paul are problematic in relationship to Genesis because of their silence regarding Sarah. A paraphrase or selected passages may be the better choice. Other texts for the day include **Psalm 22:23-31**, a song of praise for God's goodness and fulfilled promises, and **Mark 8:31-38**, one of Jesus' predictions of his death and resurrection.

# A SERMON BRIEF

Sarah and Abraham. The names evoke images of great faith and the beginnings of a people—a people who worship only one God, Yahweh. We first meet the couple in a typical-looking genealogy in the eleventh chapter of Genesis. But this genealogy is far from typical. It lists Sarai along with Abram, and makes the striking aside: "Now Sarai was barren; she had no child." When the tedious and predictable nature of a genealogy list is interrupted, pay attention; something significant is up! Not only does this list mention a *woman,* but it tells us something about her life. Sarai's barrenness raises all kinds of puzzling questions and surprises, especially when Yahweh tells her husband Abram that he will be the father of a great nation. How can the husband of a barren wife be the father of a great nation? The very hope of the Hebrew people seems doomed from the start because the mother of this nation was barren.

Nevertheless, Abram and Sarai moved along as the Lord commanded and began their adventures despite the improbability of Yahweh's promise. But what if God needed a little help fulfilling the promise? Sarai was not a stupid or shy woman. She knew what any barren woman in ancient Israel knew: bearing sons was the means to marital and social security. When she realized that she must bear a son, she arranged for her maidservant, Hagar, to bear a child with Abram. But the relationship of Sarai and Hagar ended in anger and betrayal, ending their hopes for fulfillment of God's promise through Hagar's son.

In today's reading, we find Abram already ninety-nine years old when Yahweh revisits to remind him of the promise and to establish a covenant with Abram and Sarai's family. God renames them Abraham and Sarah and promises, "I will bless her, and moreover I will give you a son by her. . . . And she shall give rise to nations; kings of peoples shall come from her" (Gen. 17:16). Abraham, like Sarah before him, has difficulty trusting God's promise and tries to find an alternative by asking God to establish the family through Hagar's son, Ishmael. But with the renaming of Sarai and Abram, God also names the son that *they* will bear. God reminds them who the real miracle worker is and promises that the covenant will be established with a son of *Sarah*.

Have you ever been in a similar situation? Where you know what God is calling you to do, but you don't see any way to make it happen? I remember receiving a frantic telephone call late one night from a friend scheduled to be married in six days. Her best friend, Sharon, had been in a tragic boating accident and was lying in a hospital bed, halfway across the country, fighting for her life. Lori didn't see how she could go through with her own wedding when her best friend might be dying. Yet, Lori knew that her marriage to Matt was part of the Christian journey that God was inviting her to take. Likewise, the doctors in that Atlanta hospital didn't know if they could save Sharon's life, much less her arm, which was badly mutilated by the accident— an arm Sharon would need to fulfill her calling to become a physical therapist. But Sharon knew better. Sharon knew God had called her to live, and to share her gift for healing and caring—especially after receiving such good physical therapy herself. Lori found the courage to trust Sharon's hope and Lori's wedding was nothing short of beautiful. And Sharon's recovery was nothing short of miraculous, as she fought back to live the life God had called her to.

Like Sarai and Abram, these women were offered chances to choose despair or hope. When Sarai and Abram were renamed Sarah and Abraham, they reclaimed their faith and chose hope. They laughed at the impossibility of the situation, but Sarah bore a child and they named him Isaac. In all of these stories, we recognize how intricately connected are God's promises and human faith. God's promises to us are not isolated events, nor are they affected solely by God's doing. We can accept those promises and participate in them, as Sarah and Abraham did, or we can turn away and try to go it alone. In this day and age, we so easily slip into inordinate pride or sinking despair. Pride can rope us in to a false sense of independence, just as Abraham had when he thought he alone could father a nation without the participation of Sarah. Such pride can happen to anyone here when you or I start thinking, "The perfect life comes when I alone earn the highest income," or "When I win the most promotions or awards I'll be happiest," or "If I save the dying earth, I'll be remembered as a great human being," or "If I can just rescue all the suffering people, I'll be a real Christian." After all, if you want something done right, you do it yourself, right? In trying to solve our problems in isolation from others and particularly in isolation from God, we begin to trust in having our slaves bear children that we can call our own. We misuse others, devalue ourselves, and fear to trust in the future. And we try to cover our abuses with an inordinate pride for having "done it on our own." Our partnership with others and with God never quite figures into the scene.

Perhaps we find ourselves swinging to the other extreme of sinking despair, related to our fear to trust in the future. Some of us find ourselves throwing up our arms, saying everything causes cancer, AIDS is incurable, Bosnia will never know peace, and politicians are all corrupt so let's vote all of them out every year! That despair is a common and honest response to our feelings of inadequacy when we try to survive alone, without a community of support or a God of love. "Don't ask me to hope for anything more loving or more just. I can survive with mediocre happiness, with a half-hearted love, with an insincere smile."

But God calls us out of that hopeless despair and out of that inordinate pride. When we trust the promises of God, we can celebrate a faith that does not rest in individualism or isolation, a promise of mutuality with God and with others as we accept our new name, the name "Christian." We rejoice in a promise that builds a community of persons working toward perfect love with God and neighbor, a community of faith, a community of hope, a community we call the church—not a stale, predictable church, but a hopeful, excited community that waits for the unexpected, participates in impossible dreams, and finds the promise of God beginning here and now. Our barrenness of distrust, injustice, fear, sorrow, and loneliness is not the end of the story. The promise of new life springing forth from dry ground can produce the fruits of right relationships, just orders, trust and faith, happiness, and community. When we respond with laughter and hope to God's promises of new life in Christ Jesus, our barrenness is renamed, our lives are reclaimed, and the promise is fulfilled.

## SUGGESTIONS FOR WORSHIP

### Call to Worship

LEADER:     Like Abraham and Sarah before us, we come hearing God's call.

PEOPLE:     **We seek this quiet time to listen with discernment and wisdom.**

LEADER:     Like Sarah, we come knowing we are barren without God's aid.

PEOPLE:     **We seek the healing to find new life in the midst of pain.**

LEADER:     Like Sarah and Abraham, we laugh at the impossible promises of God.

PEOPLE:     **We seek the faith to hope in the midst of despair.**

ALL:        **We come to worship the One who guides our search.**

## Prayer of Confession

With the saints of old, O God, we pray,
"Lord, I want to be more holy in my heart,"
But holiness eludes us.
Personal resolve,
internal fortitude, and
self-discipline fail us here.
We reach for our spiritual bootstraps
to pull ourselves up
with arms that seem too short.
Deliver us from our sin and our despair, O God.
For we cry, we sing, we pray with the saints of old,
"Lord, I want to be more holy in my heart."

## Assurance of Pardon

LEADER:     By the grace of God, we are forgiven!

**PEOPLE:     By the grace of God, we are forgiven!**

LEADER:     We are made more holy in our hearts.

**PEOPLE:     We will rejoice and be glad!**

## Benediction

LEADER:     Go forth knowing we are blessed by God.

**PEOPLE:     We carry that blessing to others.**

LEADER:     Go forth knowing God's promises are true.

**PEOPLE:     We carry those promises to the world.**

**ALL:     Let us go forth with laughter, faith, and hope!**

# Third Sunday in Lent

## *Joan SalmonCampbell*

**Exodus 20:1-17:** The Ten Commandments.

**Psalm 19:7-14:** "The law of the LORD is perfect, . . . more to be desired are they [God's ordinances] than gold . . . sweeter also than honey."

**John 2:13-22:** Jesus drives the money changers out of the temple.

## REFLECTIONS

When you look at the great cathedrals of the world, you see that they are rarely finished. They remain unfinished because of the tedium of making sure the buttresses fly just so and making sure the detailed sculpturing way up in the top of the ceiling is just so. Each detail—each rose and each petal, the statues that are all around, the angels and seraphim and cherubim—must be just so. Cathedrals are never really finished.

Now the temple in Jerusalem was larger than any of our cathedrals, and here is Jesus saying that he will raise it up in three days. Only God could do that. The people who listened to Jesus' words could not have understood what he was saying. What was Jesus implying when he said, "I will raise this temple in three days"?

In part he was suggesting that investment in our physical structures is not enough. It is important to have a place to gather and worship the Lord, but we must never be guilty of worshiping the brick and mortar instead of God. How many times have you heard of churches that get brand new space and beautiful cushions on the pews and you'd better be careful how you sit on them lest you crush the velvet? You'd better be careful not to touch the walls lest you get your fingerprints on them. It's not too different from some of our homes where we dare not live fully and completely in the whole house, for they are museums, not homes where people can feel comfortable.

When we allow the things we accumulate to become more important than who God is (as we know God through Christ), we have sinned. Jesus' anger and impatience that we see in this story become directed toward you and me.

## A SERMON BRIEF

All of us know the Ten Commandments. We've heard them, one way or another. They have guided our lives, sometimes when we've been aware of it and sometimes when we've not been aware of it. We also have other things that guide our lives and provide limits within which we can live and move and have our being.

As I was growing up, several rules were established for living in our household. My mama was full of rules, and even Daddy had to adhere to them. For example, one rule was: Always wear clean socks and underwear when you leave home. These rules were standards or norms for guiding the way we lived within the household and in the world. They were like a rule of thumb.

The expression "rule of thumb" refers to the practice of a tailor who used his thumb to measure a hem or a seam. A rule of thumb is a guide for our lives; it tells us the limits within which we can live and move and have our being. What rule of thumb establishes our social practices? What is an adequate rule of thumb for those of us in a world looking for guidance, and a sense of wholeness, meaning, and well-being?

Frequently we choose the things of the world and use them as our guide. Perhaps we hope the paycheck we wait for every two weeks or every week or once a month will give us a sense of well-being. Perhaps we think our education will give life meaning. Perhaps we allow our schedules or our social involvement to define our lives. Are these things of the world more important than God's rules of thumb? How often do we pick up the Good Book and spend time reading it to learn what God's rules of thumb are, not just the Ten Commandments but also the blessed "ares." One of these "ares," or one of God's rules of thumb, is that our bodies are temples. Jesus spoke of his body as a temple, and Paul echoes this understanding, "Your body is a temple of the Holy Spirit" (I Cor. 6:19).

Lent is a time of taking stock, of seeking to recognize the rules of thumb by which we live. Lent is also a time for again choosing to live by God's rules of thumb, God's blessed "ares."

The other day I listened to several kids from the church and the community talk about their lives. The adults sat on the periphery and listened to what the kids were saying. I was embarrassed for myself and for all parents. I began to wonder, "My God! How do I sound to my children?" The kids described how they feel every time their parents yell at them, "Why don't you go in there and clean up your room? You never do anything!" I wish you could have heard the kids as they mimicked their parents, and said things they wouldn't dare say to our faces. Kids would never say such things to us directly because we would checkmate them immediately with the rule of thumb, "You don't talk to me that way." Listen to their complaints: "We never see our parents. We don't spend time with them. There's nobody at home to listen to us. There's nobody there to talk to about our fears and anxieties about violence." These kids spent one hour and fifteen minutes talking about the violence they encounter on their way to school, after they get to school, and when they go out for recreation or to games. Living by the world's rule of thumb we parents are impatient and short; we don't have time to listen or to explain things; we are sometimes sarcastic when we offer direction.

We need a new rule of thumb, one of God's rules of thumb—we are temples. This new rule challenges us in our households and in the church to find ways to treat one another with respect, to show that we care, that we are listening. This new rule of thumb—that our bodies are temples—also encourages husbands and wives to find ways to express how much they value and love each other. I rarely see a husband and a wife touching each other and letting others see what it means when two people love each other. Are you still married after forty or fifty years? Can you give evidence that there's something good about this institution called marriage? Perhaps God's rule of thumb that our bodies are temples would allow us to demonstrate—not *over*-demonstrate—our love and affection in public. Husbands and wives, let others know that you're related to each other. Let others know that there's a sense of respect for each other. Let others know that there's a sense of respect and connectedness and valuing between you. Then children and young people might notice and want, in time, to establish a marriage covenant with someone they love.

The rule of thumb that our bodies are temples applies not only to parents and to husbands and wives but also to young people. It bothers me that a current rule of thumb is, "It's all right to live together for awhile; it's better to try shoes on before you buy them; it's all right to give yourself away and be sexually active with just anybody." It is *not* all right. It's not all right *if* our bodies are temples of Christ. Jesus' words that his body is a temple teach us to value our bodies and not let anybody do anything to make our bodies mundane and unimportant. Our bodies, our human sexuality, are gifts from

God. And we must learn how to be good stewards of these gifts, not with "thou shalt not," but rather with God's blessed "ares."

Jesus calls us to recognize that as parents, as husbands and wives, and as young people, in the social things we do we are to be concerned about ourselves and others as temples of the Lord. On this third Sunday in Lent I ask you to do an inventory. What is your rule of thumb? Young people, in spite of what you see around you, you have a mind of your own. What is your rule of thumb? What will be your rule of thumb as you live and grow?

As we take inventory, these questions are for all of us: Will we seek to know who Christ is for ourselves and live as Christ's temples, allowing the light and love of Jesus Christ to shine through us wherever we go? Will we respect others, knowing that they too are temples? Will we, like Christ, offer some good news to this broken world, God's blessed "ares"? The world has need of new rules of thumb, and Jesus counts on you and me this morning.

## SUGGESTIONS FOR WORSHIP

### Call to Worship

LEADER:      Remember the sabbath day to keep it holy.

RESPONSE:  **Let the words of my mouth and the meditation of my heart be acceptable in thy sight, my Rock and my Redeemer** (James G. Kirk, *When We Gather: Year B* [Philadelphia: Geneva Press, 1984], 58). Used by permission of Westminster/John Knox Press.

### Prayer of Confession

LEADER:      God's law is perfect; it revives the soul.

RESPONSE:  **Forgive us, O God, for we obey not your commandments.**

LEADER:      God's testimony is sure; it makes wise the simple.

RESPONSE:  **Forgive us, O God, for we place status above service.**

LEADER:      God's precepts are right; they rejoice the heart.

RESPONSE:  **Forgive us, O God, for we take delight in false gods.**

LEADER:      God's commandment is pure; it enlightens the eyes.

RESPONSE:   Forgive us, O God, for we overlook our neighbor's needs.

LEADER:     God's ordinances are true; they are altogether righteous.

RESPONSE:   O God, have mercy upon us; only you can save us. In Christ redeem us and cleanse us of sin. (Kirk, 58)

## Assurance of Pardon

Our assurance is this: "There is therefore now no condemnation for those who are in Christ Jesus. . . . For God has done what the law, weakened by the flesh, could not do." God sent the Savior, who redeems us of all unworthiness. (Kirk, 58)

## Benediction

The love of God surround you. The light of God enfold you. The presence of God guide you. Whatever you do and say, do it in the name of Jesus Christ. Go forth from this place knowing that God loves you, and so do I! Amen and Amen.

 arch 9, 1997

# Fourth Sunday in Lent

*Joan SalmonCampbell*

**Numbers 21:4-9:** Moses makes a bronze serpent and sets it on a pole, so those who have been bitten may look and live.

**Psalm 107:1-3, 17-22:** The Lord delivers those in trouble.

**Ephesians 2:1-10:** God made us alive even when we were dead in our trespasses and raised us up with Christ.

**John 3:14-21:** The purpose of God's Son coming into the world.

## REFLECTIONS

Who do these folks in Numbers 21:4-9 sound like as you listen to their grumbling? They sound like today's family. Can't you just hear them: "What'd you bring us out here for, all the way out here in this never-never land, with nothing to eat, and nothing to drink?" They're giving Moses a fit; they've forgotten that God provided manna for them. Manna—out of the sky. They woke up in the morning and what did they find? When they had nothing to eat, there was this white, flaky stuff that looks a bit like a coriander flake. They could eat it. They had more than enough to eat to be sustained on their journey. But you know, "it got old." It was kind of like leftovers. You know how folks mumble when they come home and there are leftovers on the table: "We gonna eat that stuff again?" Nobody wants the leftovers. I don't even like to put 'em in my refrigerator. So I like to say, "Eat it all up. Eat heartily."

{ 61 }

That's the same dilemma the ancient Israelites were in. They said, "You know we're tired of that white stuff. You know there's nothing really to eat here." And they'd already said to Moses, "At least if we were in Egypt we would have leeks and garlic and onions to eat. At least we would know that we'd have the juice off the soup. At least we would know we'd have the leftover crusts of bread. But you've brought us out here and there's nothing." Well, they not only insulted Moses; they insulted God. For it was by God's grace that they had something to eat. Are we like those ancient Israelites who looked (or slapped) a gift horse in the face? Do we take for granted that there are some things that we automatically ought to be able to have?

# A SERMON BRIEF

God sent the serpents to get the Israelites' attention. God allowed those serpents to nip at them. The venom from the snakes actually began to kill them. They became afraid. I tell you, I run from a little garter snake. I don't even go to the reptile house when I go to the zoo. I just don't like the way they look and the way they slither. I remember one spring I was helping my daddy move some peat moss that had been stored for a while in the garage up on the farm. Out from that peat moss came this glistening, gorgeous, black snake. Now my daddy had a cataract on one eye and glaucoma in the other, and supposedly he couldn't see. Daddy took the shotgun and shot that snake right through the eyes. I said, "Enough of that!" I was afraid that snake would nip us in the heels.

Now what's significant about being nipped in the heel? We have a very sensitive part of the body called the Achilles tendon. Have you ever had an ache there? There's no ache like an ache in the Achilles tendon. It gets your attention. You can't walk quite right. When that Achilles tendon is sore, your whole body seems to be sore.

The name "Achilles tendon" comes from an ancient Greek story. Achilles' mother was determined to protect her son from all the principalities and powers that could hurt him. She grabbed him by the heel and dipped him in the river Styx. Wherever the water touched him, he was protected. But there was one place that didn't get dipped—his heel. One of Achilles' enemies knew that this was the weakest, most vulnerable part of his body and killed him with a swift, sure arrow into his heel.

You and I have Achilles heels, literally and figuratively. Our Achilles heel is that vulnerable place in our life, the place that causes us hurt, that distracts us from remembering who God is and how powerful God is. We begin to nurse that one vulnerable spot, the thing that causes us pain, to the point that we become obsessed with it.

Let me give you some examples. All of us who have children will find at times that our children are our Achilles heels. We don't know what they're facing out in the world; we wonder what kind of choices they'll make. And we pray, Lord God protect them, Lord God walk with them, help them to make the right choices. Oh, Lord God, let there be somebody there who will listen to them and make a way for them. Then we begin to think more about the world out there than about who God is. We end up with more faith that the world can destroy them than that God can save them. Sometimes our children are our Achilles heels.

A second example is for young people. When you find yourselves worrying and wondering what you need to do in order to be popular, in order to fit in, or when you begin to think "I must please my friends and do whatever they say rather than what I know is best for me," you focus on your Achilles heel more than on God's direction for you. When you think about failing an examination or how rotten the teacher is more than you think about how God will give you wisdom and ability to understand as you study and as you take your examinations, you focus on your Achilles heel more than on God's direction for you. You can have an Achilles heel, even if you're in fourth grade.

When we in the church begin to think of all the things we cannot do because we just don't have enough time or enough money, when we do not think of what God is calling us to do in the name of Jesus Christ, we have a corporate Achilles heel.

The questions I want to ask are: "Where is your faith? Who do you believe in? Who do you trust? Who do you go to in time of need so that your vulnerable spots are protected? No human being can protect us from our Achilles heels. Only God can. To turn to God means that our focus has to be lifted from the earth, lifted a little bit higher.

You might ask why Moses put that funny bronze snake up on the pole. Because he needed to remind the Israelites to walk in faith. We, too, need to know and trust that God will guide us. Even if you have been bitten on your heel, even if your vulnerable spot aches beyond measure, you have only to lift your eyes. For as soon as those who had been bitten looked up and focused on the emblem of the snake, they were healed; they had only to lift their eyes toward heaven.

Let me tell you what happened at my church one Thursday night. There were seventy-two kids here, ranging in age from six to twenty-one. And they helped hem the purple cloth that is draped on the cross in front of the church. Many of the kids had never held a needle in their hands before in their lives. Here's how it happened. The kids just want some place to be. Sometimes they play a little basketball. At other times we talk about issues. We even do a little Bible study. Last Thursday in order to get in, they had to give me a prayer pass, a prayer request. I said to them, "If you will only make five stitches in this cloth. It is symbolic of Jesus' garments that were so filled with the presence of God that any who touched them found miracle and blessing. As you sew this cloth, I want you to offer your prayer. And when you've finished making your five stitches, say, 'In the name of Jesus I pray these things.' " At nine o'clock we all went out and draped the cloth on the cross and we prayed and they stood around the cross singing "Jesus Loves Me."

Some of those kids said, "Rev, I never prayed before. Rev, I never thought about it." Their eyes were lifted from the mundane plane of thinking that misery, trouble, and joblessness are all that's possible in life. Some thought, "I can dare lift an eye to God and in the name of Jesus Christ dare to have hope that I can find an answer to my prayer. Since that Thursday, some of those young people have called; some have come by. I see them standing outside looking at the cross. What pride they have. Their eyes have been lifted from the earth to whom and what the cross means.

What's nipping at your heels? Take it to the Lord in prayer. Dare to lift your eyes and focus on Jesus Christ.

## SUGGESTIONS FOR WORSHIP

### Call to Worship

LEADER: By grace you have been saved through faith, and this is not your own doing; it is the gift of God.

RESPONSE: **For we are God's handiwork, created in Christ Jesus or good works, which God prepared beforehand, that we should walk in them** (James G. Kirk, *When We Gather: Year B* [Philadelphia: Geneva Press, 1984], 60). Used by permission of Westminster/John Knox Press.

### Prayer of Confession (in unison)

O God, in Christ Jesus you proclaimed your love for all creation. Have mercy on us as we confess our sin. We have overpopulated the earth and violated its goodness. We have depleted nature of its vital resources. Pollution besets us, waters lie stagnant. We care not for ourselves as temples, nor for communities as buildings not built with hands. We plead for forgiveness and ask for your guidance. Help us to be disciplined in taking care of your gifts, lest in neglecting them we lose them forever (Kirk, adapted, 60).

## Assurance of Pardon

Know that God is rich in mercy. Even though we are dead through our trespasses, God's great love for us makes us alive through Jesus the Christ. We are thus saved by God's grace. Live in the assurance that, as we confess our sin, through Christ's intercession on our behalf we are forgiven (Kirk, 61).

## Benediction

The love of God surround you. The light of God enfold you. The presence of God guide you. Whatever you do and say, do it in the name of Jesus Christ. Go forth from this place knowing that God loves you, and so do I! Amen and Amen.

# Fifth Sunday in Lent

### *Nancy Hastings Sehested*

**Jeremiah 31:31-34:** "I will write it [my covenant] on their hearts."

**Psalm 51:1-12:** "Create in me a clean heart, O God."

**Hebrews 5:5-10:** Christ has been appointed by God to be a high priest.

**John 12:20-33:** Jesus faces the prospect of his death.

## REFLECTIONS

In reflecting on this ancient testimony, I identify greatly with Jeremiah. As a preacher, I know how nervous the congregation can become when the messages do not stay happy and upbeat. I am particularly aware of the incongruous picture of a southern woman preaching a prophetic word. Women are taught to "be nice." Traditionally, when we have spoken publicly in the church, it has been to offer a devotional word of encouragement. When I first started preaching from the Prophets, the congregations were caught by surprise. I have been asked by church members after a sermon from Jeremiah or Amos, "Are you angry about something?" "Are you feeling ill today?" "Have you had a bad week?" Like Jeremiah, I have wanted to respond, "Yes, you bet I've had a rough week. I've been talking to God, and God doesn't seem too pleased with the direction we're heading. As a matter of fact, I am angry that God is angry and that I have to tell you about it!" Usually though, I don't say that. I smile and say, "I'm fine." Social customs of kindness win out so often over the scandal of the gospel.

Like Jeremiah, I have wanted desperately to be liked, to receive rave reviews for my preaching. I have especially liked sticking to those "building and planting" sermons. The "pluck up and break down," the "destroy and overthrow" sermons just are not on anyone's favorite sermon list. Church members want to know why you cannot see all the good things going on in the church. Like Jeremiah, I have had times of saying, "I will not mention him, or speak any more in his name" (Jer. 20:9). Yet I speak because there is a fire "shut up in my bones" and I am exhausted from trying to find the "right," "good," "perfect," and "soothing" way to say it. With Jeremiah, I speak, singed by the fire. With Jeremiah, I am encouraged to preach a word of judgment in a time of ease. With Jeremiah, I am encouraged to preach a word of hope in a time of despair. The text of Jeremiah 31 definitely is a word of hope out of the disaster time. Hope is in such short supply these days. I am grateful for a biblical witness that can see God's hand moving out of rubble to the surprise of new life. I just hope the church can see it too.

## A SERMON BRIEF

It is time to get the family photo album down from the shelf. It is time to turn to the pages where our tribal ancestors experienced life falling apart at the seams. It was around 580 B.C. in the land of Judah. If you look closely, you will notice the pictures show a marked resemblance to our current family pictures. It was a time of cascading catastrophes. The old language and old rules of society were not functioning. A sense of safety and security was in short supply. Chaos and confusion abounded. Life was definitely out of control. Sound familiar?

Onto this scene of disaster stepped God's own chosen one, Jeremiah. As prophet and poet, with fire in his bones, he was driven by God to speak to God's people. Jeremiah's summary sermon is found in chapter 1 verse 10: "to pluck up and to pull down, to destroy and to overthrow, to build and to plant."

The Israelites clapped and said "Amen" when Jeremiah preached the "building and planting" sermons. The messages were upbeat and positive. With the good reformer, King Josiah, the people felt like they were on the threshold of a great new age. "Long live the King!" they said. But long life did not happen. King Josiah was killed. His rebellious son, Jehoiakim, worked hard then to undo all the good his dad had accomplished.

Jeremiah started preaching some "pluck up," "break down," and "destroy" sermons! The people were not impressed. They thought Jeremiah was depressed. The people advised Jeremiah to look on the bright side. They were convinced that their idolatry was easily assuaged by keeping their dues paid up at the Temple. "Long live the Temple!" Jeremiah was not convinced.

"Amend your ways!" He longed for the people to live under God's covenant. Even after all of Jeremiah's powerful and prophetic sermons, the people stayed unconvinced. Jeremiah despaired. He thought God should go pick someone else to be messenger. He scribbled some suicide notes on the back of his sermons. The fire in his bones was subject to weekly dousings. It did not take too much—a deacon's meeting or news of the new prophet search committee being formed. Yet Jeremiah preached on. He learned the freedom to speak in the face of opposition. His heart continued to yearn to speak a truth, God's truth, that would bring the people to God.

Then Jeremiah prophesied that the Temple would be destroyed and Judah would go into exile. That did it! The people were ready to fire this preacher, put him in stocks, and look for a happier, younger, and livelier preacher. The Israelites did not think destruction could happen to them. They were God's chosen, the best of all.

But destruction did happen to them. Jerusalem fell. The first exiles were taken to Babylon. Yet some of Jerusalem's leaders still refused to see. They thought they could get things back just the way they had been—with school prayer, packed pews, and no more welfare. Then the Temple was destroyed. The Temple rubble held demolished dreams for unending prosperity that was thought of as birthright and divine favoritism. Everything looked hopeless.

Jeremiah was quick to tell the hopeless that they should not blame everything on those big bullies, the Babylonians, or those right-wing folks. Jeremiah said that Israel had its priorities all messed up. Then Jeremiah drenched the people with a splash of hope. He said that everyone should take heart. God was going to forgive them and give them a second chance. Jeremiah stood on top of the rubble of Jerusalem and preached hope. He saw the disaster as an entryway to a new life.

And Jesus said: "The hour has come. . . . Unless a grain of wheat falls into the earth and dies, it remains just a single grain; but if it dies, it bears much fruit" (John 12:23-24).

Jeremiah preached that God was aware of some loopholes in the old covenant. Written laws could give someone the idea that all he or she had to do is memorize them, or make them into a pledge of allegiance. Written laws could confuse someone into believing that one could make promises with the mouth and keep one's fingers crossed behind the back.

The old covenant was tossed on the heap of rubble. God's new covenant was to be put within people and written on their hearts. This time around there would be no need for temples or texts. People would know God by heart. Doing what comes naturally would be doing God's will. No longer would people need to refer to the rule book on how to treat the stranger, the widow, the orphan, or the illegal alien. The law of God would be on their hearts. People would know by heart how to hope in the face of disaster. They would know by heart how to act with compassion in the face of hatred and violence. They would know by heart how to do justice, love mercy, and walk humbly with God.

The family album has page after page of One who knew how to live by heart. The person of the New Covenant, Jesus Christ, showed us by his life, death, and resurrection what to expect. Jesus the Christ offered us a picture of what life looks like when God's law is written on the heart.

I once saw a picture in the newspaper of a bus in Belfast. It was demolished and burned out in violence during a St. Patrick's Day festival. The bus could go nowhere to carry anyone. It was a stark image of hopelessness. But there in the picture in front of the bus a woman pushed her baby in a stroller. God's new covenant of hope was written on her heart . . . and she walked on. Out of the rubble . . . new life.

## SUGGESTIONS FOR WORSHIP

### Call to Worship

LEADER:   And God said, "The days are surely coming, . . . when I will make a new covenant with the house of Israel." The old covenant is tossed on the rubble heap of Jerusalem.

PEOPLE:   **God is making a way out of the rubble, out of the despair, out of the resignation.**

LEADER:   God's new covenant will be put within people and written on their hearts.

PEOPLE:   **We will know God by heart.**

LEADER:   God will be our God.

PEOPLE:   **We will be God's people.**

LEADER:   God's ways will be transplanted in our hearts.

PEOPLE:   **We will know by heart . . .**

LEADER:   How to hope in the face of despair.

PEOPLE:   **We will know by heart . . .**

LEADER:     How to act with compassion while the world acts with violence.

PEOPLE:     **We will know by heart . . .**

LEADER:     How to stand up for justice while the world sits down for power.

PEOPLE:     **We are the people of the New Covenant.**

LEADER     Jesus Christ, the person of the New Covenant, shows us the way.

PEOPLE:     **And we will all know God by heart.**

## Prayer of Confession

Have mercy on [us], O God, according to your steadfast love; according to your abundant mercy blot out [our] transgressions. Wash [us] thoroughly from [our] iniquity, and cleanse [us] from our sin. Create in [us] a clean heart, O God, and put a new and right spirit within [us]. Do not cast [us] away from your presence, and do not take your holy spirit from [us]. Restore to [us] the joy of your salvation, and sustain in [us] a willing spirit. (Psalm 51:1-2, 10-12)

## Assurance of Pardon

We are the people of the New Covenant. God has given us another chance. We are forgiven. We hope on. We live on, with the sure step of people who know we are God's people. Out of the rubble, there is new life.

## Benediction

Go from this place to say "yes" to the "yeses" that are in you that bring life and hope. Go with God's word written on your hearts. Covenant again to do justice, to love mercy, and to walk humbly with your God, in the name of the One of New Life, Jesus the Christ. Amen.

# Passion/Palm Sunday

## *Nancy Hastings Sehested*

*Liturgy of the Palms*

**Mark 11:1-11 or John 12:12-16:** Jesus' entry into Jerusalem.

**Psalm 118:1-2, 19-29:** The palm waver's psalm: "Hosanna!"

*Liturgy of the Passion*

**Isaiah 50:4-9*a*:** An affirmation of faith: "God helps me. . . . Who will contend with me?"

**Psalm 31:9-16:** A cry to God: "My strength fails, . . . my bones waste away."

**Philippians 2:5-11:** Christ emptied himself, humbled himself, and has been exalted.

**Mark 14:1–15:47:** The Passion narrative: from the anointing with nard to Jesus' burial.

## REFLECTIONS

I was once described as a "good preacher, though dramatic." I wonder if Jesus was ever described this way, too? Jesus was a master storyteller, offering symbols, metaphors, and images that communicated to all types of people. He had a dramatic flair for captivating listeners with his stories and parables.

The drama of the palm parade was a magnificent way to carry God's liberating message to the public arena in the power center of Jerusalem. I have wondered why the church does not follow Jesus' example of public street theater. Our time of nonviolent public demonstration in front of prisons, government buildings, and weapons factories is one way we still engage in street theater.

While preparing this sermon, I agonized over the headline news of demonstrations that have turned to violence. Demonstrations at abortion clinics have not been demonstrations of the gospel message. They have been vivid demonstrations of hatred that have sometimes turned to murder. How different was Jesus' demonstration! Passion and proclamation can go together with conviction. Yet the display of beliefs does not have to turn into a shouting match of hatred. Jesus did not force anyone to follow him on the road. His silent witness spoke volumes. He invited new ways of thinking, opening up the possibility for transformation. I thought how much we need to learn from Jesus. No matter which side of the road we stand on, Jesus offers us a powerful method of expressing gospel—visually and silently. I have wondered what it would be like if all our demonstrations were so peaceful and provocative? As Jesus' followers, where do we stand? Which way are we going? I want a ride on the donkey, don't you?

# A SERMON BRIEF

Fasten your seat belts! We are in for some sharp turns in the road during this week called "holy." If it is a holy time, how could a donkey ride of such hope and hosanna lead to a tomb of total despair? The holy has an unsettling habit of riding into our lives on some dusty and bumpy roads. This week begins with the holy drama of a demonstration march.

The march was into the holy city of Jerusalem, a city whose name means "foundation of peace." Yet it was anything but peaceful. Great tension was in the air. The Roman occupation of Judea claimed rule just before the birth of Jesus. The center of their control was in Jerusalem, the Temple City of economic, political, and spiritual power. The religious and civic leaders of the city were deeply entangled in the Roman system of bribery and corruption. The Temple had permission from Rome to collect its own tax. Once Jesus had been questioned about whether or not he would pay the half-shekel tax. Pilate, the Roman governor, had no problem dipping into the Temple treasury to fund his projects such as the new city aqueduct. And who suffered? The poor, of course. The poor were suffering terribly under the burden of taxes and military rule.

Jesus discerned the times as a *kairos* moment—a time when the city could make a pivotal choice to change its oppressive ways. Jesus chose the festival time of Passover to enter the city, knowing that the population would be tripled or quadrupled with pilgrims. Passover time was like our Christmas time for merchants, an economic boom. The need for food and lodging, plus the slaughter of eighteen thousand lambs for ritual sacrifice all made for big business gains.

Into the crowded streets Jesus made his dramatic entrance. He required a donkey to ride. Preacher Jesus assumed that everyone would quickly catch on to his street theater. The sermon for the day began on the theme of servanthood. Who could miss the show-and-tell lesson as Jesus rode on the back of a donkey? Who could miss the message of the triumphal entry of this king who slipped in nonviolently on an animal symbolizing humility? What a dramatic sermon! Only the prophets of old could compare with this act of making the message plain to a congregation.

Zechariah 9:9 speaks of God who is coming not only as "humble and riding on a donkey," but as "triumphant and victorious" as the oppressors are forced out of power. The crowd that gathered for the demonstration wanted to have their occupied country set free of Roman rule. The donkey was a beast of burden. Jesus' ride symbolically trampled not only the Roman rule, but the privilege of the high priesthood that collaborated with the foreign occupation. Jesus dramatized the hope that Israel would be a servant people, with neither Roman nor Hebrew imperialism.

Palm branches waved madly. They had been gathered from the country-side. The branches were symbols of freedom, cut down for the demonstration by people who wanted freedom the most. Waving the branches and paving the road with them recalled the Maccabean Revolt against the Syrian Empire, a time of liberation from foreign control. Shouts of "Hosanna" greeted Jesus all along the palm parade route. "Hosanna" means "save us." Jesus boldly rode toward the power seat amid the cries and hope of a people longing for freedom.

The actions of Jesus were drastic and confrontational. The disciples even tried to talk him out of them. But Jesus knew what he was doing. He was not naive regarding the consequences of this demonstration. The palm parade was a walk toward freedom, a walk that stayed firmly on the ground but with eyes staring at the heavens. The march through Jerusalem is a reminder of other marches for freedom: Gandhi's march to the sea, and the march from Selma to Montgomery. On first glance, the walks may seem like silly acts of resistance. But these freedom walks give rise to our dreams and hopes that heaven will come on earth. With hands waving, hearts pounding, and voices shouting, we find that struggle gives way to hope. Our imaginations soar into God's vision. The donkey ride that Jesus took that day was a triumph. It was a passionate proclamation that the day is coming when God's reign of peace and justice and community will ride in to stay.

Years ago, my daughter and I joined a group that demonstrated in front of the federal prison in Atlanta for the release of Cuban detainees. The prisoners shouted hosannas from their prison cells—loud cries for freedom in their native tongue, "Libertad!" My six-year-old daughter peered through the iron gates waving her small white handkerchief in response to the prisoners' desperate waves. Then she looked at me and asked, "Are we going to stay here until they get out?"

Jesus' march into Jerusalem answered her question. Yes. We are staying right here in this imprisoned land until all are set free. Hosanna!

## SUGGESTIONS FOR WORSHIP

### Call to Worship

LEADER:    Give thanks to the Lord, who is good . . .

**ALL:**        **Whose love is everlasting!**

LEADER:    Give thanks to the God of Gods . . .

**ALL:**        **Whose love is everlasting!**

LEADER:    Give thanks to the Lord of Lords . . .

**ALL:**        **Whose love is everlasting!**

LEADER:    Who performs wonderful deeds . . .

**ALL:**        **Whose love is everlasting!**

LEADER:    Whose wisdom made the heavens . . .

**ALL:**        **Whose love is everlasting!**

LEADER:    Who set the earth on the waters . . .

**ALL:**        **Whose love is everlasting!**

LEADER:    Who brought Israel out of Egypt . . .

**ALL:**        **Whose love is everlasting!**

LEADER:    Who led the chosen people through the wilderness . . .

ALL:        **Whose love is everlasting!**

LEADER:    Who remembered us when we were down . . .

ALL:        **Whose love is everlasting!**

LEADER:    And snatched us from our oppressors . . .

ALL:        **Whose love is everlasting!**

LEADER:    Who provides for all living creatures . . .

ALL:        **Whose love is everlasting!**

LEADER:    Give thanks to the God of Heaven . . .

ALL:        **Whose love is everlasting!**

## Prayer of Confession

Dear God, we have pulled along with us our unnamed sorrows and our half-forgotten dreams. We have come with weary bodies and souls from working on so many unfinished revolutions and unbendable problems. We have eaten far too many days of dry-as-dust manna. Usher us into your presence. Release us from all that hinders us from knowing you. Give us the gospel today, in the name of Jesus Christ. Amen.

## Assurance of Pardon

The liberating Son of Love has marched into our midst today. Wave your branches high! Hosanna! The One who frees all who are enslaved is with us. The One who sets the world on fire with love is among us. Hosanna! Blessed is this One who comes in the Name of the Lord! Amen.

## Benediction

Go from this place today following our Lord from the parade to the passion. And may Christ's spirit of hope go before you. May Christ's spirit of healing walk by your side. May Christ's spirit of courage nudge you from behind. And may peace catch up with you and follow you all the way home. In the name of the One who has gone before us to show us the way, Jesus the Christ. Amen.

# Holy Thursday

## Mary Lin Hudson

**Exodus 12:1-14:** The Passover story.

**Psalm 116:1-2, 12-19:** Thanksgiving to God who has "heard my voice."

**I Corinthians 11:23-26:** The Words of Institution.

**John 13:1-17, 31*b*-35:** The Last Supper.

## REFLECTIONS

With so many theologies of the Eucharist circulating, one is mindful of the potential of violating a system of belief when attempting to interpret the texts for Holy Thursday. Usually, I will select one text as the basis for my sermon, with other texts entering the field of meaning as illustrations or theological allusions that enhance the meaning of the primary text. The interplay between these texts so ignited my imagination, however, that I found myself bouncing from one to the other with creative energy. The motif of "remembrance" threaded itself throughout.

A danger in this passage is to glamorize servanthood in a way that justifies the subjugation of persons in the name of Christ. Because women have systematically been relegated to roles that require self-sacrifice for the sake of others, my interpretation of the text in John's Gospel that attempts to glorify voluntary "slavery" as a requirement for discipleship will be nonredemptive for women and for any who have endured the oppression of an unjust society. Through the use of imagination, however, one can get past the platitudes to an experience of the moment. To have a person of high status for whom you have the utmost respect suddenly stoop to wash your feet draws you into a new intimacy with that person that had not been experienced before. On the other hand, the engagement of a person of honor in that activity transforms the value of the act itself. All is made new by this radical experience. To explain is not enough. The symbolic actions must be allowed to speak for themselves. Let the congregation experience through the imagination as much of the story as they possibly can.

# A Sermon Brief

Remembrance. A time to look back. A moment to gather into the present the meaning of all that has gone on before. A sacred act of linking past to future in anticipation of another dawn. Remembrance.

The scene of solemn remembrance flashes across the screen of consciousness: The curtain rises to reveal a large family gathered at the table, resembling the slaves that once circled near the remains of a roasted lamb. With the taste of each morsel of flat bread, bitter herbs, and seasoned meat, each guest is reminded of former days of bondage, faith, and liberation. No longer do they dress for a long, strenuous journey as their ancestors did. Instead, they clothe themselves for celebration as settlers in the land of promise. What was once the "last supper" for slaves before their march to freedom becomes the "supper of remembrance" for those who have reached the destination. All are included, all are fed, all participate in the promise. Instead of preparing for another long journey at the end of the meal, a prayer is raised for the arrival of the awaited Messiah and the cup of hope is lifted in anticipation of a future of "shalom." A meal, a memory, a hope. The act of remembrance.

The scene suddenly shifts to another distant dining room, but this one bears little resemblance to the former meal. This group considers itself "family," but few blood relations can be traced. In the corner is a set of folks who have just finished gorging on a fine feast and have stretched themselves out across the furniture in an effort to relieve the effects of overstuffing. In the other corner, some of the folks are snoozing off the effects of the dinner wine that they imbibed a bit too freely. A new group of folks has just arrived after working the late shift only to find themselves standing before empty platters filled with nothing but bones and drippings. Perhaps a bit of soup might be concocted from the leftovers. But the bottles of wine have long since been drained. Someone on the couch begins to hum the familiar tune "Blest Be the Tie That Binds," but soon falls silent for lack of a second. The only thing expected of the future is the cold journey back to each individual's home and a brief night's rest to prepare for another working day. A meal? Yes. A celebration? Perhaps for some. An event that leads to wholeness and faith? Hardly.

The stark contrast between the two dinner parties is marked by the absence of memory. This second family, the good Christians from Corinth, had continued the early practice of getting together for meals as a community. Somewhere along the way, however, their memory had failed, and the story of an important meal shared by Jesus with his friends had slowly slipped away from consciousness. How else could such greed and insensitivity have overtaken the practice of "breaking bread" as a community?

The lost memory goes something like this: In a second-story room, Jesus reclined with his closest friends to share in his "last supper" before his torturous journey—a journey into the wilderness of hatred and injustice that would lead to his suffering and death and ultimately resurrection. The departure of his friend Judas was painful for Jesus and confusing for the others. Each morsel of food probably reminded them of all of the meals that they had shared, to the point that it may have become more and more difficult to swallow with each mouthful.

In the middle of it all came a startling interruption. The honored guest got up, took off his outer clothes, wrapped himself in a towel, and got down on his hands and knees and began bathing the feet of each friend who reclined at the table. A radical reversal that left each person there more than a little off balance. Like a diamond against glass, each touch of Jesus etched into the memory of those present the image of true community. From then on, as they remembered Jesus, they also remembered the awkward moment of intimacy between friends as the street grime was wiped away from the soles and ankles of their feet. In turn, their feet could never be touched by a servant again without the face of Jesus coming into view. This kind of intimacy became one measure of their discipleship. "I give you a new commandment," Jesus said, "that you love one another. Just as I have loved you, you also should love one another."

For the Corinthians to eat without regard for one another's needs was a sign that they had lost the memory of Jesus. They forgot that Jesus had reformed the significance of eating and drinking when he took the bread of the meal and later the cup of wine, and said, "This is my body, which is given for you. Do this in remembrance of me. . . . This cup that is poured out for you is the new covenant in my blood" (Luke 22:19-20). The Corinthians needed to be jarred out of their amnesia. Without their memory, they weren't linked to the earth-changing reality of Jesus' suffering, death, and resurrection, and in turn they had nothing tangible that bound them into true community with one another. They had only a platter of food and a jar of inexpensive wine that would give temporary comfort. Without the memory they had no life and no hope.

Madeline knew that it would be the last meal that she prepared for her family. Her knees were no longer reliable. Her hands shook with weakness. Her thoughts were beginning to meander away from their steady pace. She would not be able to prepare many more meals. The family knew it was hard on her and almost insisted on taking everyone out to the local cafeteria. But Madeline knew it would not be the same. She needed to feed her family one last time.

She began the baking earlier than usual. She had to sit down at the table to rest more times than she could count. As she set the long dining table with her mother's finest china, the tastes, smells, and sounds of former meals flooded her memory. Even the standard recipes called forth the voices of those who had taught her the secrets of good cooking.

As the brothers and sisters, nephews and nieces, and cousins gathered into the old homeplace, the laughter, tensions, fears and failures blended into a kind of comfortable chatter. Sisters-in-law and enlightened nephews helped transfer the dishes from kitchen to table. Finally, the time came and all sat down at their places, with Madeline at the head. She didn't say the prayer, but asked one of the brothers. All the same, she presided at the table. At that moment, the others returned—Mama and Papa, Roger and Jeannette, all the ones who had moved beyond the table. The memories of lives shared took their places around the room. Once more, in the sacredness of the moment they were family.

That spring Madeline's health declined and she moved out of the old homeplace and into a hospital bed. Within a year she was gone. At rest from teaching and cooking and cleaning up after dinner parties, Madeline passed away. It was hard for the family to gather for meals after that. The homeplace seemed so empty and the lack of coordinated schedules made it impossible to get everyone together. But finally, one day, the sisters-in-law prevailed, and the family came home for dinner once more. When the meal was prepared they all took their places; however, they sensed a presence that they had thought would never return. In her absence, Madeline was intensely present, and all she stood for took its place in the room with them. They became family once more.

Then they knew. Whenever they gathered to be family again, Madeline would always be there with them.

## SUGGESTIONS FOR WORSHIP

### Call to Worship

LEADER:     And Jesus said, "This is my body given for you."

RESPONSE:   Jesus, we remember.

LEADER: "This is the new covenant in my blood."

**RESPONSE: Jesus, we remember.**

LEADER: "If I, your Lord and Teacher, have washed your feet, you also ought to wash one another's feet."

**RESPONSE: Jesus, we remember.**

LEADER: "I give you a new commandment, that you love one another."

**RESPONSE: Jesus, we remember; help us not to forget.**

LEADER: When differences threaten to keep us apart,

**RESPONSE: Help us not to forget.**

LEADER: When violence strikes without mercy,

**RESPONSE: Help us not to forget.**

LEADER: When families huddle in hunger against the night,

**RESPONSE: Help us not to forget.**

LEADER: When women are raped and children molested,

**RESPONSE: Help us not to forget.**

LEADER: When enemies hurl slurs of hatred,

**RESPONSE: Help us not to forget.**

LEADER: When heavy pain is hard to bear,

**RESPONSE: Help us not to forget.**

LEADER: When hearts seem shattered beyond repair,

**RESPONSE: Help us not to forget.**

LEADER: "I do not call you servants, but I have called you friends. I'm giving you these commands so that you may love one another."

RESPONSE:   Jesus, we remember. Remind us again, that we may not forget.

## Prayer of Confession

Welcoming God, you blanket the earth with the invitation to dine as your guests at the feast of life. You call us to friendship and community with the intention of healing our brokenness. Yet, we have offered excuses for not joining in. We claim unworthiness rather than accepting your favor. We honor correctness more than we value relationship. We strain to uphold the bitter walls of class, race, and gender so that we might not be shaken by another's pain. Forgive us, O God. Wash us thoroughly that we may be a part of your life. Open our eyes to the new creation that awaits our presence. Draw us together in the memory of the One who walked into death for the sake of life, even Jesus our Leader. Amen.

## Assurance of Pardon

The invitation has not been revoked. The offer is extended again and again. "Come and eat." Today's opportunity awaits. Love one another as Christ has loved you. Live in joy for you are forgiven.

## Benediction

Go in peace to live in love. Remember the words, the face, and the touch of Jesus, who called us to be family to one another. And the forgiving grace of God will enfold you and uphold you in the hope for a day when all people will join hands together and sit down at the table of friendship to dine in joy.

# Good Friday

## *Mary Lin Hudson*

Isaiah 52:13–53:12: Song of the Suffering Servant.

Psalm 22: The Cry of Dereliction.

Hebrews 4:14-16; 5:7-9: We have a high priest who "has been tested as we are."

John 18:1–19:42: Jesus' betrayal, trial, crucifixion, and burial. Peter's denial.

## REFLECTIONS

Many Good Friday services in which the account of Jesus' arrest, trial, and crucifixion is read will not permit a lengthy sermon. The purpose of proclamation is to connect the scandalous story of Jesus' suffering with the pain and brutality of the present world. There is plenty of material available about present suffering—just pick up a daily newspaper in any metropolitan area. More than that, however, the suffering of Jesus connects with the lives of those who shared Christ's purpose, but whose work threatened to change society in radical ways. The deaths of these martyrs convey the senseless waste of good people of value, and in so doing, inform the story of Jesus with contemporary meaning. It is here, in turn, that Jesus' story can offer the accounts of martyrdom a glimpse of hope for a future transformed by the power of God.

In *The Prophetic Imagination,* Walter Brueggemann argues that "the royal consciousness leads people to numbness, especially to numbness about death.

It is the task of prophetic ministry and imagination to bring people to engage their experiences of suffering to death" (Philadelphia: Fortress, 1978, 46). This calls for a language of grief with which to call forth the pain and terror within us. Once the preacher can call forth the reality of pain and fear within the congregation, then there is room for newness to emerge. In Brueggemann's words, "weeping permits newness to come" (60). That is a primary motivation behind this sermon.

# A SERMON BRIEF

The horror of the scene refuses to fade. A twenty-year-old Salvadoran worker dressed in a torn nightshirt is led by three men to a hill of garbage on the outskirts of town. The evidence of beatings, rape, and torture scar her face and legs. She turns in silence to face the barrel of a military rifle that fires a fatal bullet into her forehead. In humiliation and defeat, her body is discarded as one more object to be added to the huge mound of refuse that society has tossed aside.

This scene from the movie *Romero* depicts the unlimited brutality of political leaders in their efforts to crush the movement for justice and freedom among the disenfranchised of their land. At the same time, the film reminds us that the abandoned bodies and the drained blood of these visionaries are not lost, but are invested in a future hope for a world of shared abundance and a creation at peace. This movie also contains the words of Father Oscar Romero, another Salvadoran martyr: "I've often been threatened with death. If they kill me, I shall arise in the Salvadoran people. Let my blood be a seed of freedom and a sign that hope will soon be a reality."

Christians gather to review the horror of Jesus' crucifixion year after year on a day we call "good." We read aloud of the arrest, the interrogation, the trial. The shouts of the mob ring out anew. The mockery of soldiers and the scorn of witnesses come to life as the story unfolds. We wait and watch as Jesus hangs between two criminals on a desolate hill outside the city. We listen for his final breaths; we feel his pain. And in the silence of death, we mourn, but not too deeply. No sense in getting too upset over Jesus' death when we'll be singing "Alleluias" in less than forty-eight hours.

Perhaps only those who have carried the corpses of the dead can fully comprehend the horror of the crucifixion: those who have called out for their sisters—Maura, Ita, Dorothy, Jean—only to find the lifeblood of these religious workers spilled out onto the roadside of the Salvadoran landscape; those who held the hemorrhaging head of a brother called Martin, a leader who dreamed of children, black and white, living together hand in hand; and those friends of sisters Agnes, Barbara, Joelle, Shirley, and Kathleen, now buried in a field in Liberia, shot dead in a civil war "because they had white skin." For those who mourn the dead, the crucifixion of Jesus retains its horror.

And yet the killing continues. Lies and hatred lead to violence, while truth is saddled with blame. Competition for power strikes down the innocent. Rulers seek to silence the voice of freedom out of fear that it will awaken the cry for justice among the oppressed. Brothers and sisters are considered enemies, not family. The world is weary with war. Must this go on forever?

Perhaps we have grown numb under the strain of senseless violence. Perhaps the "Alleluias" of Easter are as hollow as our observance of Good Friday because we have no deep need of hope in God's future for creation. Until we are wounded by the grief of the world, we cannot hope for God's new life to transform it. We must tear through the anesthetized layers that shield us from the horror and brutality around us, and reach into the place where we can still be touched by suffering. Let yourself feel the injury of pain. Let yourself weep.

After I had served the Lord's Supper to my home congregation (a rare occasion), a woman I had known for many years came up to me and said with tears in her eyes, "Each time I eat the bread and drink from the cup, I remember my son, Bill, who was shot down in Vietnam." Broken body, shed blood. Jesus' passion draws into itself the suffering of the whole world.

Mothers, weep for your children! Weep for the death of your children! And know that the mother of Jesus weeps with you.

Cry out, my friends! Cry out for the vindication of the blood of your sisters! Moan and wail for loss of your brothers! Let the suffering of the innocent find a voice in your prayers for the coming of the day when the suffering, the death, and the violence will come to an end. Hear the voice of Jesus groaning in agony with you. How long, O Lord, must we bury our children in early graves? How long before nations can lay down their weapons and join hands in peace? How long before the blood of the martyrs will spring up in the freedom of the poor and imprisoned? How long, O Lord, how long?

# SUGGESTIONS FOR WORSHIP

## Call to Worship

LEADER:     Whom are you seeking?

RESPONSE:  Jesus of Nazareth.

LEADER:  The one handed over by his own disciple, arrested by police, questioned by religious leaders and tried before Pilate?

RESPONSE:  Yes, Jesus of Nazareth.

LEADER:  The one flogged by soldiers and mocked by officers; unjustly sentenced and convicted by a crowd of his own people?

RESPONSE:  Yes, Jesus of Nazareth.

LEADER:  The one who carried his cross to the place of the skull and hung there between two criminals; whose clothes were divided among gamblers and whose side was pierced by a spear?

RESPONSE:  **Yes, Jesus of Nazareth—despised and rejected. By his brokenness, we are made whole. By his bruises, we are healed.**

## Prayer of Confession (in unison)

All we like sheep have gone astray; we have all turned to our own way. And the Lord has laid on him the iniquity of us all.
Lamb of God, who takes away the sins of the world, have mercy on us.
Innocent One, who takes away the sins of the world, have mercy on us.
Truth Incarnate, who takes away the sins of the world, have mercy on our souls.

## Assurance of Pardon (Isa. 53:5 adapted)

He was wounded for our transgressions. He was bruised for our iniquities. The chastisement of our peace was upon him and by his stripes we are healed.

## Benediction

The blood of Christ, fallen to the ground, now mingled with the blood of martyrs, seeds the earth with freedom that will one day rise to fill all creation with the beauty of justice and peace. Weep for those who have suffered, and let the seeds of hope be planted in your heart this day.

# Easter Day

## *Mary J. Scifres*

**Acts 10:34-43:** Peter testifies to Cornelius.

**I Corinthians 15:1-11:** Paul testifies to the Corinthians.

**John 20:1-18:** Peter's confession.

**Mark 16:1-8:** The women are sent out from the empty tomb with the good news.

## REFLECTIONS

**Acts 10** records Peter's preaching on Christ's resurrection and commission to the disciples. This could be coupled with the song of victory and proclamation of God's power in **Psalm 118** for a message on our response to the news of the resurrection.

**I Corinthians 15** is an interesting counterpoint to either of the Gospel lessons since all of the Gospels, written later than Paul's letters to the church at Corinth, record the women as the first resurrection witnesses. Since Paul's list of resurrection appearances excludes women, this text might point to the persistent importance of women despite early church prejudice.

**John 20** is a late account of the resurrection focusing on Mary Magdalene, thus providing a tender picture, almost poetic, of the special relationship between Jesus and Mary, a possible springboard for a sermon. The juxtaposition of the men's running against Mary's weeping might also provide interesting sermon material. In today's sermon, however, the focus is on the response to the resurrection: to believe (Mary) or not (Thomas); to understand (Mary) or not (Peter).

**Mark 16:1-8** is thought to be the original ending of this Gospel. A sermon could explain that this ending pushes the reader back to Mark 1:1 to recall the story again and again so that we might learn to live the story of Jesus' life and passion, continuing the journey for understanding what it means even in the midst of terror and amazement. Such a controversial sermon could be enlightening for many congregations and a comfort to those who struggle with doubts but are embarrassed to name them.

# A SERMON BRIEF

Have you heard the news today? Mary hadn't heard it when she found the empty tomb. All she knew was that someone had stolen the body of her beloved teacher and mentor, Jesus. But when a "gardener" appeared, Mary expected to hear where the body had been taken. Instead, she heard a familiar voice call her name, and she recognized that her friend and teacher had risen from the dead. Can you hear it? Jesus has risen, Christ is alive, we have all been saved.

Even though the church calendar invites us to remember the resurrection every Sunday when we worship together, many of us would rather celebrate Jesus' birth every week. After all, which songs do we yearn for all through December? Which holiday includes gifts, parties, festive church events? For many people, it's obvious that Christmas is the holiday of choice. And it *is* a wonderful day, a day to celebrate the arrival of the Messiah, God's promised child to lead us, the Christ who would save the world.

So, why are we so hesitant to rejoice in the celebration of that day of salvation, the day of resurrection? Have we not heard the message? Jesus has risen, Christ is alive, we have all been saved. Or have we heard a message that doesn't excite us because we just can't believe it? Commentaries consistently note how difficult it is to find a new twist on the Easter message since we're preaching to people who have heard it all their lives and live it every week. But we Christians have trouble living and believing it every week, even if we have heard it many times. After all, if Christ is alive, then we ought to be living differently. No more "life as usual," or "daily routine." Mary recognized that immediately when she went to the disciples to announce that she had seen Christ and he had a message for them. Are we afraid to believe? Afraid of the changes such belief might force us to make?

Are we afraid of the connection between Jesus' life and ours? Are we afraid to believe, afraid to face up to a world that is far from the reign of God that Jesus proclaimed? We may be afraid, but we worship the God of strength, the God of comfort, the God of love who promises that our fears will not be the final word. Hear the good news: Jesus has risen, Christ is alive, we have all been saved. Yes, that means things have changed. But hear the changes: Death is no longer the powerful force it once was. And sin no longer has an unbreakable hold on our lives. Our behaviors are no longer controlled by these two formerly powerful forces of sin and death.

But do we *really* believe that we are free from death? Examples abound of our fears and denial of impending death: deathbed cries for a few more years to perfect this life; lifetime obsessions with cosmetic ways to deny the aging process; drunken birthday bashes to ignore the reality of another passing year; refusals to plan for our deaths through wills, trusts, funeral preplanning. We are terrified of the inevitable fact of life that we will die, seldom giving a second thought to the fact that our under-used Christian beliefs offer us a promise of new life that conquers death.

Do we believe that Christ has overcome sin in our lives? Examples of disbelief abound here as well: teenagers who condemn themselves for not living up to their parents' expectations; constant picking at our inadequacies while ignoring the gifts that God *has* given us and uses in our daily work; demeaning ourselves about the five pounds we gained on vacation; parents blaming themselves for every problem in their children's lives; churchgoers thinking they never do enough; people drowning with regrets for failed relationships. We can't seem to find that new freedom that life in Christ promises.

But this freedom is real. And with this freedom comes the responsibility to live that good news and to share that good news, just as Mary did when she proclaimed Christ's appearance to the disciples. It's no secret society we're a part of. We are the church and are called to invite others to be a part of this Body of Christ. We have heard the good news. Jesus has risen, Christ is alive, we have all been saved. Can you hear it? Can you share it with others? Are you ready for the changes that belief in him brings? Does it have the power to excite you?

Mary wasn't ready. She was looking for a dead body, looking to offer her last respects. But then she heard a voice, saw a man, and recognized Christ when she heard her name. Christ calls each of us by name. Listen . . . Christ is calling each of us. Can we answer that call? If a young Galilean woman in first century Palestine could hear the call and evangelize twelve stubborn men, convincing them that the message of Jesus was not lost, then surely we can do the same.

We are a resurrection people. Let's celebrate that as we accept this good—no great—news! We can find that Easter excitement because Jesus *has* risen, Christ *is* alive, we have *all* been saved!

## SUGGESTIONS FOR WORSHIP

### Call to Worship (Ps. 118:24)

LEADER This is the day that the LORD has made.

PEOPLE: **Let us rejoice and be glad in it.**

LEADER: On this day, the first day of the week, at early dawn, the women went to the tomb, taking the spices they had prepared. And they found the stone rolled away from the tomb.

PEOPLE: **Hallelujah!**

LEADER: And the women departed quickly from the tomb with fear and great joy. And behold, Jesus met them and said, "Hail!"

PEOPLE: **Hallelujah!**

LEADER: And Mary stood weeping outside the tomb. And she said, "They have taken away my Lord, and I do not know where they have laid him." Saying this, she turned around and saw Jesus standing, but she did not know that it was Jesus. And Jesus said to her, "Mary." And she turned and said to him, "Dearest Teacher."

PEOPLE: **Hallelujah!**

LEADER: We are witnesses to these things, and we know that we worship a risen Lord.

PEOPLE: **Hallelujah!** (adapted from *The United Methodist Book of Worship*, no. 396)

### Prayer of Affirmation (in unison)*

God of rainbows and resurrection, you are our strength and our salvation. We have entered your gates today to sing songs of praise and joy, proclaiming your victory over death on this day. In doing so, you have lifted all of us from the hands of death and delivered us for lives of righteousness. We shall not

---

*Please note that many traditions dispense with the Prayer of Confession for Easter worship.

die, but shall live, but we pray for your grace and courage to believe and proclaim that Jesus has risen, Christ is alive, we have all been saved! Amen (adapted from Psalm 118).

## Benediction

LEADER:  Why have we wept? Jesus has risen!

**PEOPLE:**  **We are no longer weeping. Christ is alive!**

LEADER:  We need not wander, for Jesus has called to us;

**PEOPLE:**  **And we have called him by name. Christ is alive!**

LEADER:  God has commanded us to go to our brothers and our sisters and proclaim the good news.

**PEOPLE:**  **We have all been saved. Christ is alive!**

# Second Sunday of Easter

## *Barbara Bate*

**Acts 4:32-35:** The early Christian community's unity.

**Psalm 133:** The psalmist celebrates unity.

**I John 1:1–2:2:** "If we walk in the light . . . we have fellowship . . . and the blood of Jesus his Son cleanses us from all sin."

**John 20:19-31:** The story of doubting Thomas.

## REFLECTIONS

The heart of this set of readings is, for me, the image of the oil coming down over the beard, collar, and robe of the priest in Psalm 133. My experience of Eastertide is also expanded as I envision working among the Acts 4 community, where individualism and competition are absent and biblical hospitality takes over. I kept thinking of the images of oil and the community, and I found myself surrounded with other images of smiling, laughter, and movement.

My own congregation is a joyful one. Hugs are frequent each Sunday, and the music in its small sanctuary often includes black gospel or liberation songs from the 1960s and '70s. As I continued to work with the texts I realized that the passage about Thomas was interesting to me only in the final affirmation, since my own experience of recent times leaves me assured rather than doubting. So the psalm and the passage from Acts were the energy sources for this particular Sunday.

Only after I had begun the sermon brief did I remember the friendship cake and the face of Frances. The fact that we know each other across the apparent boundaries of race and class made the gift of the cake a powerful experience for me. I can't wait to share it with other people when the cake is ready to serve!

# A SERMON BRIEF

I had never heard of a friendship cake before this past Christmas. I had received cakes and sometimes prepared them for other people, mostly for birthdays. But because I'm always trying to get myself to eat less dessert, I rarely make cakes for my small household. I hear the voice calling, "Oh sugar, sugar," too easily.

The idea of the friendship cake came in an unexpected way, from Frances, an African-American woman of sixty or so who cleans up the office where I work. We were talking one day as I finished my afternoon cleanup and as she began her evening's work. I asked where she went to church, and found out that she had begun that day making more than a dozen different items for the bake sale at her congregation. One of the items was a friendship cake.

Frances said it takes a month to prepare three friendship cakes, using a series of fruits, nuts, and cake flour, and that you have to begin with starter of fruit and sugar from a previous month's recipe. "Would you like some starter? I'll be doing the next cakes after the new year."

I've been working on the cake during the same time as I've been thinking about the first-century Christians. "No one claimed private ownership of any possessions, but everything they owned was held in common. There was not a needy person among them" (Acts 4:32, 34). That image of living in connection with one another makes me long for a situation in which people do not buy everything as conspicuous consumers but find ways to share their goods, their time, and their identities as beloved children of God.

Many years ago I worked in a community action agency in which a colleague of mine, Toni, talked about the life in the inner-city neighborhood in which she had grown up. No one was rich, she said, but when a fire occurred in a neighboring apartment many people helped within twenty-four hours by bringing food and furniture, and by caring for the small children in the household. Several years later, when she and her family moved into a larger apartment in the less densely populated part of the city, another fire occurred. That time there was no immediate help from neighbor to neighbor. Toni simply heard one resident say to another, "I hope they have insurance."

It would be wrong to idealize the caring that people give to one another in conditions of hardship. What is given by members of a community is not just material help, but affirmation and celebration.

Psalm 133 makes the celebration visible and vivid. The oil spills over the beard, the collar, and the robes of the holy one. You can almost watch the grin and hear the laughter. How can we not grin and laugh in the face of the great joy of Easter! Unfortunately, it is possible to rush past the moment of joy and think only of a single act of resurrection.

Close your eyes and imagine the oil dripping over the head and neck and collar of the priest's robe. Or, if it is easier, imagine yourself in a shower, surrounded with warm water and steam. Can you also imagine singing your favorite song, or listening to someone you love singing a favorite song?

The laughter, oil, water, and singing are all ways to give vent to the senses as windows into celebration. Eastertide is more than a moment. It is a direction, away from being stuck and toward being swung into action.

In some congregations the Sunday after Easter is a low ebb in the church year. It is as if the finale has been staged and the curtain has nowhere to go. On the other hand, seeing the Easter event as the opening of a grand celebration allows both the pastor and the people to go forward into the community as people revitalized and reminded of who they are and who they have come to enjoy and to serve. Each Sunday is a reminder of the resurrection life of God's people. We can follow members of Eastern Orthodox congregations in beginning every greeting with the words "Christ is risen," followed by the words "Christ is risen indeed."

Where is a friendship cake being prepared in your own figurative kitchen? Where are the fruits of your soul being sweetened and combined to bring forth food for a community celebration?

The idea from both the Acts community and the priestly ritual of the oil is free of individualism and competition. Laughter, grins, and hugs are the stuff of Easter. Allowing the Easter season to go forward is possible in the spirit of "pass it on, and have a wonderful time!" Delight does not cancel out problems, but it makes them possible to bear together.

The power of the friendship cake lies in its roots—its being given by another—and its dailyness—its requirement to be stirred up daily and replenished with a variety of ingredients. I cannot gather a successful "starter," bring about the basic delight, all by myself. I also cannot make a good recipe without a variety of ingredients, and a recipe. It's friendly because it depends on me to be a friend and on others to be available to be recipients of a tasty cake.

One danger in the Jesus story is to consider only Jesus, forgetting that Jesus loved others, taught them, challenged them, forgave them. Especially in the season of Easter it is tempting to give the whole "plot" to Jesus and to forget how crucial were the listeners, the proclaimers, and even the doubting ones such as Thomas who had to see Jesus' nail marks for himself before he could celebrate the risen Lord as his own. The images of the church community in Acts and the Psalm that is virtually "gooey with thanksgiving oil" are vivid reminders that community and the gospel are one.

# SUGGESTIONS FOR WORSHIP

## Call to Worship

LEADER:    Thanks be for Easter,

**PEOPLE:    for Christ who has risen,**

LEADER:    with blessings of life all around;

**PEOPLE:    laughter of children,**

LEADER:    dancing in worship,

**PEOPLE:    soaring of eagles,**

LEADER:    rebirth of nature,

**PEOPLE:    justice envisioned,**

LEADER:    love amid difference,

**PEOPLE:    good news for the frightened,**

LEADER:    food for the hungry,

**PEOPLE:    home for the stranger,**

LEADER:    blessings expanding our world.

**ALL:        Thanks be for Easter, for Christ who is risen!**

## Prayer of Confession

It's easy to put away the Easter decorations, Lord, and simply to hope that we'll keep alive the celebration for longer than a day or two this year. But it's hard to keep that resolution when the joy is crowded out by the old conflicts in the workplace, the household, or the city. It would be wonderful to believe that this time Easter peace really did break out in the world that is so full of war. It would be wonderful to believe that the hands of Thomas really did touch the wound in our spirit and heal it.

I commit myself to the belief in the Jesus story, despite the clutter of past thoughts and present occupations. I give myself to the recognition of disillusion and the open window of hope. I give myself to the continuing possibility of new life and connection in a community of faith. And finally, I give myself to the gift of my own life, renewed in the service of love and justice, your gift of shalom.

## Assurance of Pardon

You are God's beloved, forgiven in the spirit, and given in love. Be at peace, and be joyful. Amen.

## Benediction

God brings forth good gifts to each one who lives in God's spirit. Go forth in the delight of a resurrected life, and in a community set free to be an eternal gift to our world. In the name of the One whose love has no end, Amen.

# Third Sunday of Easter

*Penny Zettler*

**Acts 3:12-19:** This miracle is illustrative of the life and power to be found in God. Those watching and questioning are invited to know the truth, that salvation comes from Jesus Christ so that their lives may be filled with the "times of refreshing"—times of peace—that come from the Lord.

**Psalm 4:** This psalm begins with an aggressive insistence that our prayers be answered. It concludes with the assurance that, with God, and only with God, it is possible to have peace in any circumstance.

**I John 3:1-7:** The focus is on being children of God as opposed to children of the dark. Our sins have been forgiven and we have a new identity because of God's great love for us.

**Luke 24:36*b*-48:** Jesus' words are the gift we long for—the gift of peace. All that has transpired in Christ's life to this point was so that he could give this gift to his followers—"Peace be with you." Our peace is God's grand plan and design.

## REFLECTIONS

The common thread in the texts is the issue of having peace with God, peace as children of God. Peace is a gift from God and can be found only in God.

Do women ministers have a particular sense of peace and contentment? Do women pastors have a greater need to sense peace and contentment? If our lives as women are more complicated by doubling up tasks than those of men in our culture, do we need to hear the message of peace more clearly?

As I move through my days as mother, wife, daughter, pastor, teacher, preacher, counselor, gardener, and cook, the people I love want cookies, kisses, a word from God, advice about marriage, teaching on the Second Coming of Christ, and dinner. It is so easy to feel overwhelmed by the demands to live double time. Peace.

How deeply I need to hear this word before I speak it. In our turbulent world, our people's needs are as great as our own.

## A Sermon Brief

I think some of us who grew up in the church forget what a treasure we have in being called children of God. We forget the great chasm that separates children of the light from the children of the darkness. I think often I go about my life as if it didn't really make that much difference. But it makes a difference, a life and death difference.

Perhaps if we could see what it really means to live as children of the darkness, we would more fully treasure our lives lived in the warm, joyful, bright light of Jesus' love.

Perhaps only a few times in life do we get to see the chasm that separates that life choice. It's always an eye-opener and a heart stopper.

My family and I sat in the rental car and my husband asked again, just a little louder, "Honey, are you coming or not?" After months of negotiation and planning we were in the vacation spot from hell.

I had arranged this fabulous family dream vacation. Because we have access to free air travel and great German first cousins, we could get the family to Europe for a steal.

I loved the planning, figuring, and strategizing of the dream trip. The planning was almost as good as being there would be. We had only disagreed over one tourist stop.

The trip would be complete with castles draped with fairy-tale moats; restaurants smelling of sauerbraten, sausage, and spetzle; great cathedrals adorned with rich stained glass; and quaint villages where cows with loud clanking bells drink from the central water fountains. We'd have desserts of rich, wonderful, German chocolate and then throw in a few more castles.

But no death camps. Definitely no death camps. My husband thought that it would be good for the kids to see Dachau. He said that after all it was an important part of history. He mentioned the educational value of being in such a place.

I argued that we all see enough darkness in a week at home so to choose a place of horror for a sunny morning's vacation tour seemed particularly insane—even if it were to benefit the children.

Actually, I was revolted at the thought of being in a death camp. I was physically sick to my stomach at the thought of being in a place where so much chaos and evil had been free.

But here we were, having driven through the proper, prim, perfect, German countryside. The day was full of blue skies and white powder-puff clouds. We had driven past scenic little houses with starched lace curtains—windows overflowing with pink and red geraniums. And here we were in Dachau, this place of darkness splotched onto the shiny countryside.

"Are you coming?" he asked again. I got out of the car and walked through the gray chain-link fence into that place of evil. I slowly caught my breath and took in Dachau, the death camp where so many of God's best creation were exterminated.

It was dark. Gray. Devoid of color. There had been absolutely no attempt to put a smile on what had happened here. No one was pretending that what had occurred had not. There were no German geraniums brightening up the scene. No white lace curtains on any window.

The paths were dirt. The buildings were worn, gray, rough wood. The sculptures were black iron. The pictures were black and white. The names of those murdered were written on the walls in black ink. A plain gray sign pointed to the area where the ovens were, where so many were murdered and not given so much as a funeral shroud.

In the place where God's heart broke, there were only images that continue to bring tears. Only darkness.

It was so satisfying. So right!

It was such a perfect picture of a world that did not know God, a place where chaos reigned and the children of the darkness were, for a short minute, allowed to have power.

Is evil gray? Maybe evil is no color at all. Darkness covers up the delightful things of God like pink, iridescent purple, canary yellow, or white. These worlds are nothing alike. They are light-years apart. As different as night and day. As different as good and evil.

Now I've seen what evil looks like. I've also seen what God's world looks like in all its purity after a snowfall, underneath a spring rain shower, and bathed in a rainbow.

Would that I could see the contrast more clearly day to day. It would make my choices easier.

# SUGGESTIONS FOR WORSHIP

## Call to Worship (I John 3 adapted)

LEADER:  Behold what manner of love our God has poured out upon us.

**PEOPLE:  That we should be called the children of God.**

LEADER:  Beloved, we are God's children now.

**PEOPLE:  It does not yet appear what we shall be.**

LEADER:  **But we know when Christ appears, we shall be like him.**

**PEOPLE:  For we shall see him as he is.**

LEADER:  And those who have this hope in Christ are purified.

**PEOPLE:  Even as Christ himself is pure.**

## Prayer of Confession

Loving God, we come this morning as your children. We come as little children come from playing in the dirt this week—oh, we're cleaned up on the outside, so others can't see the mud; but we're not very well cleaned up on the inside. We forget that that's what matters most.

Forgive us for the mud slinging we've been part of this week, the slovenly way we have forgotten to do the simple kindnesses, the filthy selfishness we gravitate toward so quickly, the soiled habits we clutch so tightly.

Loving Father/Mother God, scrub off our hearts and make us clean on the inside. Wrap us in your warm, tender arms and let us know that we have purity, healing, and peace with you. Amen.

## Assurance of Pardon (Acts 3:19 adapted)

If we repent and turn from our sins, the scripture tells us our sins will be blotted out and we will receive from the Lord "the times of refreshing."

## Benediction

God's peace be with you,
the peace that passes all understanding,
the peace that comes only from and through the God of
peace—who gives peace to us all to move out into a world of chaos
with confidence and joy.
God's true, deep, and abiding peace be with you. Amen.

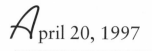

# Fourth Sunday of Easter

*Penny Zettler*

**Acts 4:5-12:** Salvation, healing, life itself is from God through Jesus Christ. This is the basis of our faith—salvation is found in no one else.

**Psalm 23:** This is a prayer poem of comfort. It celebrates God who acts in love on our behalf, through all the times and situations we encounter. It is not just love in words but care and sustenance for rich, real, abundant life here and now and into eternal life ever after.

**I John 3:16-24:** To look at Jesus is to see what love really looks like. John writes to his dear children about the practical issues in the Christian life and answers the question: How do we know if we are really loving one another? The answer is to look at our actions and see if they match the self-sacrificing action love of Christ.

**John 10:11-18:** Jesus gives his life willingly, in love for those he shepherds. We are his and his great love for us is seen by the gift of his life to restore our relationship, to save us from alienation and death.

## REFLECTIONS

The texts are linked by the astonishing action love of God. There is no place in God where love is not an action, a deed. Love initiated by God is seen as God's care, gifts, and life offered for God's children.

Women are often so busy acting out love that they can hardly catch a breath. As we love our congregations, our lives may seem pushed to the limit by the action love with which our lives swirl. In my ministry I am often surprised by how those actions start out as love gifts from my heart and end up as tasks in which I am over my head, and resentful of those I am serving.

The nurturing, caring gifts I can offer in ministry relationships are in need of hearing the constant call to sacrificial love born out of the depth of my love relationship with God. I need to regularly let God remind me of God's gift that I am privileged to offer to others: a gift that results in balanced, joyful ministry that is full of God's love—and mine.

# A SERMON BRIEF

How do you know somebody loves you? No, not hope, or wish, but really, really know—absolutely to the bottom of your being. Not by what they say, or even by what they give you. I suppose we all know that the most sure way to know you are loved by someone is to watch the way they treat you—the way they act. The way they act, when things go right or, maybe more important, when things go wrong.

I always knew my parents loved me. I never doubted that. But if someone had asked me how much they loved me, I wouldn't have had a way to measure the size of their love—until the summer when I was sixteen.

That summer my family vacationed with another family in the mountains of northern Arizona. My family stayed in the other family's cabin and did all the tourist things in the area. One afternoon my sister, her friend, and I begged to go horseback riding. I was the one with the brand new, shiny, driver's license—my proudest possession. My parents easily gave permission for me to drive our very fancy, luxury car to the horse stables. I was dependable, trustworthy, yes, even a Girl Scout! I could be trusted to do the right thing.

As I drove up and up the mountain I remember wondering at the odd choice of location for this horse stable. It was smack on top of a huge mountain. But I had no problem getting up there. I drove confidently up the winding road and parked carefully in the tiny parking lot on top of the mountain. We rode the horses and had a grand time, until it was time to go home. Then the three of us piled into the car, and I began to think long and hard about just how we were going to get back down off that mountain. It hadn't taken much effort to get up there, but I could see that I was in lots of trouble now that we needed to get down.

There was just no room to turn the huge, fancy, luxury car around in the tiny, dusty, parking lot. I tried maneuvering back and forth. No luck. No way. I certainly couldn't imagine backing down the mountain; my driving skills weren't nearly that well developed. As we sat in the car and tried to figure out what to do, one of the people who worked with the horses came over and offered a wonderful piece of news. He said that there was another way down the mountain—another road and it was right in front of the car! It was a little-used road but would get us down just fine. I was delighted. No turning, no backing—just down.

I started the car forward with confidence. I could see that the road wasn't as well used as the one on which we had come up the mountain, but I was so glad to have a way out of trouble that I didn't give that much thought. Things were great for the first few car lengths, but as I drove, the road very quickly began to get bumpy. Then even more bumpy. More bumpy than any road ought to be. There were rocks in the road that gave way to larger rocks and even some boulders. I tried to avoid the largest rocks but there were too many to outmaneuver; rocks began to scrape and rip the bottom of the car. About halfway down the mountain I became convinced that if this had ever been a road it certainly wasn't one now. I could hear car parts being dropped on the mountainside.

I stopped the car to try to think of another way out of this terrible mess. I couldn't see anything to do but to go straight forward, down the mountain, and finish this terrible experience. I glanced around one more time to see if there was any other way out and as I looked full circle I saw my parents standing, with their friends, watching me drive the car down the side of the mountain.

I was sick. I put the car back in gear and finished driving, scraping, and leaving car parts as a trail behind us. The adults watched.

I drove the car over to where my parents and their friends were standing. I couldn't imagine what was going to happen. Before I could even stammer out an apology, an explanation, or put any words to my repentant tears, my father's friend said furiously, "If she were my kid . . . " His face was red with fury over what had been done to our family's car. My father interrupted him, put his arms around me, and said, "She didn't mean to."

We rode back from vacation in the broken car, with no air-conditioning and not much spunk, but neither were there any recriminations. I was forgiven. I knew how much I was loved! More than money, more than comfort, more than I would ever deserve! More than a big luxury car, more than other people's comfort, more than mere words. I was loved truly.

How do we know we are loved?

I can so easily be tricked into thinking that if I say the right words, and wave the magic wand verbally, I can shortcut the action needed to give comfort and stay in true, loving relationship with those around me. But the actions always speak so much more loudly than the words. Certainly we all need to hear the words, too, but words without action drain away the nothingness. Put some action with the words and the message is loud and clear.

So the word became flesh . . . and we have as our ultimate example of love Father God, Mother God, loving parent God, taking me back after I smash the car, wreck the relationship, spoil the job, ruin my life. God offering me life and life and life again through action-proven love.

## SUGGESTIONS FOR WORSHIP

### Call to Worship

LEADER:    By this we know love, that Christ laid down his life for us.

PEOPLE:    **Let us not love in word or speech, but in deed and truth.**

LEADER:    This is God's commandment, that we should believe in the name of Jesus Christ and love one another.

PEOPLE:    **For all who keep these commandments abide in God, and God in them.**

### Prayer of Confession

Loving God, we come together, as people who don't really even know how to be together. We come claiming to be your people but knowing that underneath it all, we are never deserving of your love. So often we expect your love and care for us to be like ours for those around us; and we know we fall short of loving you, our brothers and sisters, and ourselves.

Remind us that your love is far more tender than we ever dream. Love us back to you this morning. Love us back into the shape you have for us—holy, and whole and lovely. God of love in action, who has already acted in love on our behalf, accept our confession and fill us again with your spirit of love. Amen.

### Benediction

Go confidently knowing that you are loved.
Go securely trusting that you are filled with love.
Go joyfully empowered to love
and to release the power of love in your world!
In the name of our loving God. Amen.

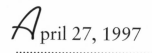

# Fifth Sunday of Easter

### Nancy Lambing

**Acts 8:26-40:** The story of the Ethiopian eunuch: "What is to prevent me from being baptized?"

**Psalm 22:25-31:** A celebration of God's sovereignty: "All the ends of the earth shall . . . turn to the Lord."

**I John 4:7-21:** A singable text: "Since God loved us so much, we also ought to love one another."

**John 15:1-8:** Jesus' teaching on spiritual interdependence: "I am the vine, you are the branches."

## REFLECTIONS

Preaching on love is both a breeze and a challenge. There are endless songs, poems, and stories on love. People of all ages have an understanding of love. That's the breezy part! The challenge comes in finding a fresh approach to a familiar topic.

I chose to develop this sermon in an interactive style. Since everyone knows love in some way, this style allows people to participate and claim the message. I allow the congregation to respond to the questions. My congregations are used to this approach and participate readily. Initially, I assured them there were no right answers and I was not looking for something in particular.

My understanding of the purpose of the sermon of I John is this: to convince the hearer that God's love is known in the real-life person of Jesus

Christ. Other themes that could be developed include: abiding/living in love, what it means to love boldly, perfect love casts out fear, and the role of the Spirit.

# A SERMON BRIEF

There is a billboard that I see regularly. It reads:

> HATE AND RAGE
> ARE FOUR LETTER WORDS.
> SO ARE
> HOPE AND LOVE.

Have you seen it? Have you heard about it?

Love. A four letter word that is used to describe our relationships with everything from food to fun to friends and family. Have you known love?

Love. A feeling that we all experience toward something.

What do we love? (I allow the congregation to respond.)

I love popcorn and sewing. I love my children, my husband, and God.

As human beings we love a variety of things. We love a lot of foods, things, and people. Surely we don't love our friends the same way we love a good movie. Certainly we don't love chocolate the same way we love our dog. There are a variety of kinds of love—puppy love, young love, first love, perfect love, true love. We love a lot, and we love in a variety of ways.

But before we ever loved—before we ever cared—God loved us. Love is from God. This is true love.

I remember the first Sunday school song I ever learned:

> Jesus loves me! This I know,
> for the Bible tells me so. . . .
> Yes, Jesus loves me!
> Yes, Jesus loves me!
> The Bible tells me so.

Perhaps this was one of the first songs you learned as well. This song reminds me that from the very beginning God has loved us and loves us still. The Bible tells us so. Remember that first Bible verse you learned? For many of us it was John 3:16:

"For God so loved the world that
he gave his only Son, so that
everyone who believes in him may not
perish but may have eternal life."

That's true love.

"Have you not known? Have you not heard? Has it not been told you from
the beginning" (Isa. 40:21)?

Yes, we have known God is love! In songs, in scripture, we have known
God's love for us.

What are some other ways you've known God's love? (I allow the congregation to respond.)

Yes, we have known God's love through the hands and hearts of others.
Love lived out in hands is true love. We have experienced love through
handshakes, smiles, and hugs. We have literally experienced love through the
flesh. We have known love through those who have been bold enough to
express love.

Thank God for those bold enough to love. Praise the Lord for people bold
enough to hold our hand when others have slapped it. Thank God for the
ones bold enough to hold us when we are sick. Thanks be to God for those
who boldly speak out for us on our behalf. Yes, we have known God's love!

Love comes to us in the flesh. In the same way, God's love has come to us
in Jesus Christ. Jesus Christ was sent as God's love in the flesh. Through Jesus
we know that love is not merely a concept or an idea, but real and true love.

We have known God's love in the love Jesus lived out so boldly when he
didn't punish the woman caught in adultery; when he provided wine so the
wedding party could continue; when he called out to the bent-over woman
and straightened her up; when he invited the children to be near him; when
he touched the lepers; and when he enjoyed the perfume poured on his head
by a woman.

The same love that so boldly abides in Jesus and in others abides in us
through the Spirit. We have known God's love when we felt too weary to
love, only to become energized. We have known God's love when we were
powerless, only to become strengthened. We have known God's love when
we felt too faint to love, only to be given power.

We have known God's true love when, in our weakness, we have found
the boldness of love. There are times when each one of us runs out of the
energy to love others. There are times when we are too tired, too busy, or too
selfish. At those times, God comes to us loving us so that we might love one
another.

But God doesn't love us just so we can love others. God loves us because
God has created us. And God expects us to love ourselves. When Jesus was

asked about the greatest commandment, he responded: "The first is, . . . 'you shall love the Lord your God with all your heart, . . . .' The second is this, . . . 'love your neighbor as yourself' " (Mark 12:29-31). Most of us are better at loving others than we are at loving ourselves. Women especially are better at loving others. This message of I John teaches us that true love is God's love *for* us.

True love from God is a grace-filled love. It is not a result of our love for God. We love, because God first loved us. That's hard for us to comprehend. We are so used to working to get ahead, studying hard, sacrificing ourselves and our families. First John reminds us that we don't have to earn our love from God. God has loved us from the beginning. In Jesus Christ, true love has been made known to us.

"Have you not known? Have you not heard? Has it not been told you from the beginning" (Isa. 40:21)? God has loved from the beginning, through the flesh of divinity and through the flesh of humanity. This love has been graciously poured out on us and flows through us. So, then, beloved, let us love one another, because love is from God.

## SUGGESTIONS FOR WORSHIP

### Call to Worship (from Psalm 22)

LEADER:        From God comes my praise in the great congregation;

LEFT SIDE:   From God comes my praise in the great congregation;

RIGHT SIDE: From God comes my praise in the great congregation.

LEADER:        Those who seek the Lord shall praise the Lord.

LEFT SIDE:   Praise the Lord!

RIGHT SIDE: Praise the Lord!

LEADER:        May your hearts live forever!

ALL:              May your heart live forever!

### Prayer of Confession (from Psalm 22)

LEADER:        Listen to the cries of the hungry . . . , the lonely . . . , the refugees. . . .

PEOPLE:     My God, my God, why have you forsaken me?

LEADER:     Hear the voice of the woman with AIDS . . . , the pregnant teen-
            ager . . . , the abused child. . . .

PEOPLE:     Why are you so far from helping me, from the words of my
            groaning?

LEADER:     Incline your ear to the sounds of the sick . . . , the tired . . . , the
            workaholic. . . .

PEOPLE:     O my God, I cry by day, but you do not answer; and by night,
            but find no rest.

LEADER:     Eternal God, hear our voices:

ALL:        We cry out on behalf of all your people suffering and in need.
            Forgive us for hearing their voices and turning away. We have
            not acted out of your love and compassion. We have not loved
            others as you have loved us.
            Open our ears that we might hear.
            Open our hearts that we might abide in your love.
            Open your hands that we might hear, love, and act.
            In the name of love we pray. Amen.

## Assurance of Pardon

LEADER:     From the beginning, God has loved us.
            "There is no fear in love, but perfect love casts out
            fear; for fear has to do with punishment" (I John 4:18).

PEOPLE:     Thanks be to God for loving us, casting out our fear, and setting
            us free to love.

## Benediction

May the true love of God, the compassionate presence of Jesus the Christ,
and the boldness of the Spirit abide in our hearts and hands today and always.
Amen.

# Ascension Day

*Barbara Brown Taylor*

**Acts 1:1-11:** The book begins with a reference to the contents of "the first book" and picks up the story with Jesus' charge to the apostles to wait in Jerusalem for the baptism of the Holy Spirit. This is followed by a description of Jesus' ascension; he is "lifted up and a cloud took him out of their sight."

**Psalm 47:** This psalm is a celebration of God's sovereignty: "Clap your hands, all you peoples!" or Psalm 93: This psalm is a hymn to God's majesty: "The Lord is robed, . . . girded with strength."

**Ephesians 1:15-23:** The writer gives thanks for the faith of the Ephesians. He prays that the eyes of their hearts may be enlightened, that they may know "the immeasurable greatness of (God's) power" which was accomplished in Christ when he raised him from the dead and seated him at his right hand in the heavenly places." All things, the author emphasizes, have been put under Christ's feet.

**Luke 24:44-53:** The Gospel ends with its own version of the ground covered in the first several verses of Acts.

## REFLECTIONS

The story of the Ascension in the book of Acts ends with a promise from the two men in white. "This Jesus, who has been taken up from you into heaven, will come in the same way as you saw him go into heaven" (1:11). Technically speaking, we are still waiting for that promise to come true, which may give us another clue to why Ascension Day is so ignored. Who wants to celebrate being left behind? Who wants to mark the day that Jesus went out of this world, never to be seen again? Hungry as we are for the presence of God, the one thing we do not need is a day to remind us of God's absence.

A friend of mine came back from a trip to England with a story about Our Lady of Walsingham, an Anglican church famous for its fifteen chapels. Each one commemorates a different moment in the life of Jesus and his disciples, beginning with the Annunciation and ending with the day of Pentecost. Each is decorated with familiar symbols of the event it remembers—stars and magi in the chapel of the nativity, a wooden cross in the crucifixion chapel, an empty tomb in the chapel of the resurrection.

My friend was having a fine time, he said, until he came to one chapel that was curiously unadorned. Looking around, he found no clue as to which chapel he was in until he looked up and saw two bare plaster feet with nail holes in them hanging out of the bottom of a plaster cloud. Of course! He was in the chapel of the ascension. There was nothing at eye level. Just those wounded feet way up there above him, disappearing into the cloud over his head.

That is the felt truth of Ascension Day—the experience of being left behind—and it offers the preacher a powerful opportunity to speak to those who sometimes feel abandoned by God. The sermon does not have to remedy this situation in order to deliver good news; it has only to tell the truth so that people recognize themselves in what they hear from the pulpit. Depending on the preacher, the congregation and the time in their communal lives, Ascension Day may also provide an opportunity to talk about the new life that becomes possible after the death of an old relationship. In Luke 24, the disciples return to Jerusalem "with great joy." When we lose those we love, we may discover that their absence allows them to be present to us in a new way.

# A SERMON BRIEF

The problem with preaching on Ascension Day is that few people know or care what the day is about (including many preachers). Yes, it is one of the seven major feast days of the church year. Yes, what happened on that day is an article of faith in both the Nicene and Apostles' creeds. But ask a hundred people which event in Jesus' life they remember best and chances are you won't get a single ascension. It is simply not part of most people's canon.

Every other act of his life has a human dimension to it. His birth, his bar mitzvah, his friendships, his miracles, his tears—even his death and resurrection have the feel of real human experience about them. We know something about these things. We have tasted these things in our own flesh and blood. It is not until he leads his followers to the Mount called Olivet and floats out of their sight forever that most of us—literally—lose track of him.

Where did he go? Why did he go? How did he go? Nothing remotely like this has ever happened to any of us. No one else travels in clouds. No one else sits at the right hand of God.

Ascension Day is not about us. It is about Jesus alone, and that can make it slippery to handle. Like the disciples, our only part in this drama is to stand on the ground with our mouths hanging open, wondering what in the world to make of it all.

The inaccessibility of the Ascension can work against a preacher. It can also work for her, if only because she has so little furniture to rearrange. Very few people have preconceptions about the Ascension, other than the obvious up-and-down view of the universe. As much noise as we make about how God is in here with us and not out there somewhere, "up" is only a problem for the literalists among us. In the symbolic language of faith, "up" is as good a direction for God as any. We lift up our hearts, after all.

We confess Christ is risen. We raise our hands in praise and thanksgiving. Remember how wonderful it was, when you were three feet tall, to be lifted up over the heads of grown-ups?

Up is where he went, according to Luke. Matthew does not say a word about it, and Mark is vague at best. "So then the Lord Jesus, after he had spoken to them, was taken up into heaven and sat down at the right hand of God," he writes in the last couple of verses of his Gospel, the ones we are not even sure he really wrote. John suggests that it happened on Easter Day. "Go to my brothers and say to them, 'I am ascending to my Father and your Father, to my God and your God,' " he says to Mary of Magdala outside his tomb, but that is the last we hear of it (John 20:17). Instead of ascending he goes to cook breakfast on the beach for his friends, and when John's Gospel ends he is still going strong.

Luke is the most peculiar of all. On Ascension Day we hear both of his accounts—the one he used to close his Gospel and the one he used to begin the book of Acts. That makes sense, since that same story is both the last chapter of Jesus' life on earth and the first chapter of the church's. What does not make sense is that Luke cannot seem to decide how it happened, exactly. The first time he tells it, it happens on Easter evening in Bethany, but the second time he tells it, it happens forty days later on the Mount of Olives. Maybe he heard it both ways and did not want to choose. Maybe the story changes as people repeated it, depending on whether they saw it as the end of Jesus' ministry or the beginning of their own.

In either case, the relationship to Pentecost is clear. As inaccessible as it may seem, the Ascension is still about flesh and blood—that is, about us.

Symbolically speaking, Jesus ascended in order to finish what he had begun with us. It was not enough that through him God was born into the body of the world. That was just his Christmas gift to us. His Ascension gift was that through him the body of the world was borne back to God. By presenting his own ruined, risen body to be seated at the right hand of God, Jesus imported flesh and blood into those holy precincts for the first time. He paved the way for us, so that when we arrive after him everyone there will not be quite so shocked. He restored the goodness of creation, and ours in particular. By ascending bodily into heaven, he showed us that flesh and blood are good, not bad; that they are good enough for Jesus, good enough for heaven, good enough for God. By putting them on and keeping them on, Jesus has not only brought God to us; he has also brought us to God.

He got out of the way in order to set us on our ways. Once he arrived in heaven, he turned on the faucets of the Holy Spirit and drenched his scared friends, who became his body on earth. They were good for nothing as long as they stood staring into the sky. When two men in white robes appeared and asked them why they were doing that, they reconsidered. They looked at each other instead, and what do you think they saw? Peter saw his brother Andrew, James saw his brother John, Thomas the Twin saw Simon the Zealot, and James, son of Alphaeus, saw Judas, son of James. Matthew saw Philip and Philip saw Bartholomew. They all saw each other, and all together they walked back to Jerusalem and devoted themselves to prayer with one accord. With nothing but a promise and a prayer, those eleven people consented to become the church and nothing was ever the same again, beginning with them. The followers became the leaders, the listeners became the preachers, the converts became the missionaries, the healed became the healers. The disciples became the apostles, witnesses of the risen Lord, and nothing was ever the same again.

That probably was not the way they would have planned it. If they had had it their way, they would probably have tied Jesus up so that he could not have gotten away from them, so that they would have known where to find him and consult him forever. Only that is not how it happened. He went away—he was taken away—and they got on with the business of being the church. The Lord who was not anywhere anymore had become everywhere instead. It was almost as if he had not ascended but exploded, so that all the holiness that was once concentrated in him alone flew everywhere, and the seeds of heaven were sown in all the fields of earth.

That is the heart of the story. It is still waiting to be embodied, which is difficult to do when the body in question has just floated out of sight. A preacher has at least two clear choices on this day: to deal with what is happening in heaven in a purely imaginative way or to keep her feet planted realistically on the ground. The first option allows for sound theology by way of playful speculation. (What do the angels smell on Jesus when he arrives? What is the most shocking thing about him? What do they like best about him? How does his humanness change heaven's perspective on earth?) The second option sticks closer to human experience and must deal with the fact of Jesus' absence.

Almost every church with stained glass in it has an ascension window. In it, Christ hovers in the air, his hands upraised in blessing, while the disciples look up at him with something between awe and delight. But he is there with them—he is in the window—and if they appear joyful then we may assume it was because they thought he would be back in a day or two, next week at the latest.

Two thousand years later, we tend to see the whole thing a little differently. We need another window, a modern one, to describe our own situation: a window with just us in it—no angels, no Jesus, no heavenly light—just us, still waiting, still watching the sky, our faces turned up like empty cups that only one presence can fill.

In many ways, our worship services are how we have organized our waiting. We come to acknowledge the Lord's absence and to seek the Lord's presence, to sing and to pray, to be silent and to be still, to hold out the empty cups of our hands to be filled with bread, with wine, with the abiding presence of the absent Lord until he comes again. Historically and theologically, this is the work of resurrection. Jesus' death and disappearance result in the birth of the church. He has gone away from us, and even this is good news.

## SUGGESTIONS FOR WORSHIP

### Call to Worship (based on Ps. 51:15, 10, 12)

LEADER:     Open our lips, O Lord,

PEOPLE:     **And our mouths shall proclaim your praise.**

LEADER:     Create in us clean hearts, O God,

PEOPLE:     **And renew right spirits within us.**

LEADER:     Cast us not away from your presence

PEOPLE:     **And take not your Holy Spirit from us.**

LEADER:     Give us the joy of your saving help again,

PEOPLE:     **And sustain us with your bountiful spirit.**

## Prayer of Confession

Almighty God, our heavenly Father:
We have sinned against you,
through our own fault,
in thought, and word, and deed,
and in what we have left undone.
For the sake of your Son our Lord Jesus Christ,
forgive us all our offenses;
and grant that we may serve you
in newness of life,
to the glory of your name. Amen.

## Assurance of Pardon

May the Almighty God grant us forgiveness of all our sins, and the grace and comfort of the Holy Spirit. Amen. (*The Book of Common Prayer* [New York: Seabury Press, 1979, 127-28.])

## Benediction

Glory to God, whose power, working in us, can do infinitely more than we can ask or imagine: Glory to God from generation to generation in the church, and in Christ Jesus forever and ever. Amen (based on Eph. 3:20-21).

# Day of Pentecost

## *Barbara Brown Taylor*

**Acts 2:1-21:** The Pentecost story.

**Romans 8:22-27:** The Holy Spirit intercedes for us.

**John 15:26-27; 16:4*b*-15:** Jesus promises to send the Counselor.

## REFLECTIONS

Pentecost is a festival shared by Jews and Christians, whose calendars are very similar at this time of year. While Christians celebrate Easter, Jews celebrate Passover, both of which are calculated by the moon. Fifty days later, Christians celebrate Pentecost as the birthday of the church while Jews celebrate it as the day of commemoration for the giving of Torah at Mount Sinai. In Hebrew, the day is Shavuot, which (along with the New Year, the Day of Atonement, Tabernacles, and Passover) is one of the five holy days of the Jewish year.

I mention this because it seems to me that Pentecost is more than an opportunity to celebrate the great variety of expression in the Christian family. It is also an opportunity to celebrate the great variety of expression in God's worldwide family. When the tower of Babel collapsed, human language shattered into a thousand odd-shaped shards and human beings encountered the limits of communication. On the day of Pentecost, that trend was reversed. God did not give us back one language, but we received the ability to understand one another across the cultural borders that had until then contained us.

This seems truer and truer in the world today, as fiber optics bring us face-to-face with our neighbors around the world. English is a second language for many of those neighbors, whose lives are becoming as familiar to us as ours are to them. Paperback book clubs advertise three volume sets on Sufism, Zen Buddhism, and Taoism. Schoolchildren learn about Gandhi as well as Mother Teresa. Some fear this signals a universalism in which all of our flavors are boiled down to thin broth. Not necessarily. It may also signal our Pentecost ability to listen to one another and to hear God speaking to each of us in our own languages.

The same thing goes for our own communities. When we, like the first disciples, leave our forts to share our fire with the world, it is imperative that we listen. If we insist that everyone speak our own language, we will miss much of what God has in store for us. Instead, we may learn to speak some new languages ourselves—so that we can talk to people who have lost their faith or who never had any, or who have experienced God in a different way. Was the miracle on Pentecost the speaking or the hearing? For those whose heads are on fire with the love of God, the answer is: both.

# A Sermon Brief

The church year is split nearly in half, like a circle with a line drawn across the middle. It is a year that begins with Advent in late November, arching upward through the high seasons of Christmas, Epiphany, Lent, and Easter before dropping back down below the horizon for the long, eventless months of summer and fall. Traditionally, the first half of the year is known as Jesus' season, and the second half as the season of the church. Pentecost is the feast day that marks the transition between the two.

On Easter, we celebrate the resurrection of the Lord. On Pentecost, we celebrate the birthday of the church, which is also a resurrection—the transformation of a bunch of frightened disciples into the apostolic founders of the church, thanks to the gift of the Holy Spirit. The festival was a Jewish one to begin with, a harvest festival that brought Jews from all over the civilized world to the temple in Jerusalem. They had to go. It was one of three obligatory feast days of the year, and so they went: Medes and Elamites from the east; Romans from the west; Libyans from the south; and Cappadocians from the north—all of them streaming into the city and setting up their own camps, so that walking through the crowded city was like taking a trip around the world, with Arabic singing over here and Libyan laughter over there and the smell of Egyptian food cooking over an open fire wafting over it all.

There was only one group missing—the small band of orphaned disciples, who were not walking the streets at all but who were huddled together behind closed doors for fear of their enemies. They were dead, for all practical purposes—leaderless, powerless, visionless—the sole survivors of a catastrophe that had robbed them of their future. The world had become a frightening place for them and they had barricaded themselves against it, believing that their only safety lay in sticking together and keeping everyone else out.

If things had happened differently for them, they might have gone on that way, establishing a church that was essentially a hideout, a place for threatened, like-minded people to get together and agree on everything that was wrong outside while they held themselves apart from the baffling world in which they lived. They might have decided that only their own descendants could belong to the church, and that even they would have to pass certain tests before being allowed to enter. They might have kept everything they learned from their Lord to themselves, using all the fuel he gave them to keep their own stove warm.

But that is not how things happened for them. When the day of Pentecost arrived, Luke tells us, the Holy Spirit invaded their hideout and set them on fire. One by one, God turned them into human candles, giving each of them a flaming crown to wear and when they opened their mouths to say to each other, "Hey! Watch out! Your head's on fire!" what came out instead were strange languages, languages none of them had ever learned in school. It sounded like pure gibberish to them until the great noise they were making drew a crowd and travelers from all over the world began to arrive, looking like a delegation from the United Nations—some of them wearing fine Roman togas and others in the long flowing robes of the desert, some with homespun tunics and others in animal skins—all of them leaning through the doors and windows of the hideout to hear themselves addressed in their own tongues.

And this was just the beginning. The next thing that happened was that the onlookers accused the disciples of being drunk, and Peter took advantage of the situation by telling them all about Jesus of Nazareth, so that all who heard him were cut to the heart, and said to the apostles, "Brothers, what should we do?" and Peter told them. "Repent, and be baptized." So they did—three thousand of them that very day—and there was not enough room for all of them in the hideout anymore, which was just as well, since what became clear that first Pentecost day was that the church was not supposed to be a hideout anyway. It was supposed to be an outpost of heaven, a convention of human candles—all those set-on-fire and breathed-on ones— sent forth by the same Holy Spirit who would continue to breath on, in, and through them until they filled the whole world with God's heat and light.

That makes Pentecost a kind of Easter for the church. Fifty days ago we celebrated the resurrection of our crucified Lord. Today we celebrate the resurrection of the church that was crucified with him. For a little while his followers wandered in the wilderness and wondered what to do without him and considered staying behind shut doors forever, but on the day of Pentecost a mighty wind blew the "Keep Out" sign off the front door of their fort and they all spilled out of it, with lit faces and the tongues of angels. Alleluia, the church is risen! The church is risen indeed, alleluia!

A couple of years ago my husband, Edward, and I went walking in Spain, where we ended our trip at the medieval cathedral of Santiago de Compostela. In the fifteenth century, Compostela was the third most holy city in the world, right behind Jerusalem and Rome, and pilgrims streamed into it from all over the place—some of them by boat, some on horseback, most of them on foot—to say their prayers at the place where the bones of Saint James, patron saint of Spain, are said to be buried.

While their numbers have dwindled, they are still at it today. I stood in a long line to put my fingers into the roots of Jesse's tree, which is carved into the marble column that supports the statue of Saint James at the front door of the church. It is the traditional way of thanking God at journey's end, and so many people have done it over the centuries that they have worn five deep, shiny holes into the solid rock. After I had done my part to make them a little deeper, I wandered into the huge, gilded interior of the church and mingled with everyone else—tourists wearing cameras around their necks, nuns fingering their rosaries, pilgrims moving their lips in silent prayer, and people pushing wheelchairs in hope of a miracle—all of us milling through that holy space like visitors to one of the courts of heaven.

Then some acolytes appeared at the altar and began lighting candles, so I slid into a pew. The service was in Spanish, of course, so I understood almost none of it, but on the other hand I understood everything. I knew the shape of the service by heart, and when it got to the places I recognized—like the confession, or the Creed, or the Lord's Prayer—I just said it in my own language, and I was not the only one. I heard some German behind me, and French off to the side. A couple of rows ahead of me there were people from Asia who I am pretty sure were not speaking Spanish.

It did not seem to matter what language any of us spoke. Standing to sing, kneeling to pray, and holding out our hands to be fed, we knew that we were worshiping the same Lord, and halfway around the world in a foreign land we found ourselves at home.

This is an absolute miracle, if you ask me, that a faith born in a little sliver of a Middle Eastern country two thousand years ago has made it all around the world, so that the mighty acts of God are praised today in Swahili, in Turkish, in Maori, in Vietnamese—all of us curling our tongues around different words that translate into the same reality: one Lord, one faith, one baptism, one God and Father of all.

It all started on the first day of Pentecost, when John the Baptist's promise finally came true. Those who huddled there that day were washed not with water but with the Holy Spirit and fire. It was God's gift to them, but more important, it made them God's gift to the world. Their baptism by fire was not for their own spiritual renewal, but for the renewal of the whole world. Pentecost is God's cure for all whose spirits have grown dim and whose tongues are tied. The burned out are set on fire again, by the power of the Holy Spirit.

## SUGGESTIONS FOR WORSHIP

### Call to Worship (based on Ps. 126:1-3)

LEADER:     When the Lord restored the fortunes of Zion.

PEOPLE:     **Then were we like those who dream.**

LEADER:     Then was our mouth filled with laughter,

PEOPLE:     **And our tongues with shouts of joy.**

LEADER:     Then they said among the nations,

PEOPLE:     **"The Lord has done great things for me."**

LEADER:     The Lord has done great things for us.

PEOPLE:     **And we are glad indeed.**

### Prayer of Confession

God of all mercy,
we confess that we have sinned against you,
resisting your will in our lives.
We have not honored you in ourselves, in each other,
and in the world that you have made.
Reach out your saving arm
and rescue us from our sin.
Forgive, restore, and strengthen us
through our Savior Jesus Christ,
that we may abide in your love

and serve only your will
for your people and all creation. Amen.
(*Supplemental Liturgical Texts: Prayer Book Studies 30* [New York: The Church Hymnal Corporation, 1989], 64-65.)

## Assurance of Pardon

Almighty God have mercy on you, forgive you all your sins through the grace of Jesus Christ, strengthen you in all goodness, and by the power of the Holy Spirit keep you in eternal life. Amen. (*Supplemental Liturgical Texts,* 64-65.)

## Benediction

May the God of hope fill us with all joy and peace in believing, through the power of the Holy Spirit. Amen (based on Romans 15:13).

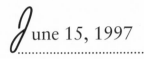

# Ordinary Time 11 or Proper 6

## *Loida Martell-Otero*

**I Samuel 15:34–16:13:** Samuel anoints David to be King.

**Psalm 20:** Davidic psalm celebrating divine help for the anointed.

**II Corinthians 5:6-17:** We walk by faith, not by sight.

**Mark 4:26-34:** Parables about the kingdom of God.

## REFLECTIONS

My father, who was a top-notch baker before entering the pastorate, would often repeat the following dictum after baking a particularly good-tasting cake: "It's all in getting the right formula. If you have the right formula, everything works out perfectly." It struck me that this is an underlying philosophy by which many live: We seek to know the right formula, so that everything will work out perfectly. The modern Western world is particularly addicted to seeking the "right formula" as part of its bias for all things "scientific." Western Christian theology has also fallen prey to this predilection: we seek to find the exact "how-tos" of a good religious practice and of successful church leadership. But is this search for such a formula justified? Is there a key for leadership and renewal in our churches today? I would posit that in II Corinthians 5:17 God is challenging the church today not to seek formulas for success, but to live, as Martin Buber expressed, "in abiding astonishment," in awe and wonder at what God has done in our midst through Jesus Christ.

# A SERMON BRIEF

It is interesting that as popular as the word "renewal" has become, it is not a common New Testament term. This is because of the church's early understanding of itself and of its mission; that is, it saw itself not as renewed but as a completely new community.

It saw itself as a community born of the Spirit and under God's reign. In this New Age that Jesus Christ had inaugurated, people were no longer enslaved to sin or death; "the proud were scattered" and the powerful were brought down from their thrones. Clearly, the old formulas for leadership had changed. This was a new society that strove to live God's vision for all of humankind.

The apostle Paul reminded the early church, in his second letter to the Corinthians, that more than a community, it was a Body. In this Body, no one was dispensable. Each contributed to the health and integrity of the Body. The blind were made to see, lepers were not held afar but embraced, the oppressed received good news of their liberation. This new community lived conscious of the powerful presence of God in their midst. Knowing who was Lord and what was required of them, this transformed community lived such that "all who believed were together and had all things in common" (Acts 2:44). As the Spirit blew, the old barriers of age, gender, ethnicity, and social class were swept aside—all were one in Christ Jesus. The old formulas did not work; those who sought to be first learned to be last. As the disciples struggled with issues of power and authority and even leadership, they were confronted with the newness of God's reign. They learned from Jesus that leadership was defined by service and love to others. They were confronted by Jesus' own life and witness, that he made the supreme sacrifice of service and "[gave] his life [as] ransom for many" (Mark 10:45). Service was the result of love for the neighbor, but neighbor was no longer defined as the person next door, the "kindred spirit," the one who looks like me or is agreeable to me. Neighbor was now the enemy, the stranger, the one who is not in my community or my sphere of comfortableness. All expectations were shattered, all formulas thrown to the wind in this new community. We can perceive throughout the New Testament writings, particularly in the book of Acts, a church filled with excitement and energy. This church understood itself to be a sign of the Kingdom, a light unto the world, a piece of "tomorrow" brought to life today.

What made the difference? There were two critical events: the Cross and the Spirit. The Spirit is the giver of new life, the Spirit of God in action. This "ruach," this wind that blew in creation, is the Spirit that not only anointed Jesus as he inaugurated a New Age, it is also the Spirit that participated in the re-creation, the birth of this new community. At Pentecost, we see the once-frightened and weary transformed; the silent speak. This newly empowered, dynamic community became a witness to God's salvation. They now announced the good news: God reigns! But there was a catch. For the Spirit to come, Jesus had to go to Calvary (John 16:2). Jesus died at the Cross, vanquished sin and death, and resurrected as the Risen Christ who then breathed on his disciples and said, "Receive the Holy Spirit." The Spirit came, in wind and fire, on Pentecost and forever changed the course of human history. It is this understanding that leads Paul to proclaim joyously: "So if anyone is in Christ, there is a new creation: everything old has passed away; see, everything has become new"(II Cor. 5:17)!

Today, our churches are buffeted from within and from without. We face the daunting issues of homelessness, poverty, and economic despair. We must deal with the realities of racism and sexism, domestic violence, sexual abuse and battery. It seems that nature itself is at war. In these telling times, the church struggles and many have lost hope. We struggle to be faithful to God, even as we sense that somehow we have lost the way. We seek renewal. We want to be restored. The question is, restored to what? We want to be restored to that sense of mission and empowerment that characterized the early church. Can it happen? Is there a formula that will make it all perfectly right? To experience renewal we must again struggle with two realities: the Holy Spirit and Calvary.

To speak of renewal is to invite the Spirit to come once again into our midst. Some might say that the Spirit is already in our midst. The question, however, is "Who is exercising the Lordship?"

We seek the presence of the Spirit, but we seek to be in firm control of it. When the Spirit blows, one is born anew, in the power of the Spirit, and one has no control over where one is to go or where one is to stay (John 3:8). What a frightening thought for so many! What about our strategic planning or long-term goals? What about our neat formulas? The Word of God is clear: If all things are to be new, all things must be subsumed under the Spirit of God. A pastoral colleague shared this insight with me: "The hardest thing in the world is to give our lives to Christ as Lord, because when we do, all our fears and control issues come to the fore. That is why we need to convert every day."

Which brings me to Calvary. Even as the Spirit comes because of Calvary, so we must go the way of the Cross to experience the Spirit's renewal. Second Corinthians not only states that all things are made new, it emphatically states that "everything old has passed away." *That* is the problem. We want to experience renewal without Calvary, without letting go of the old. We have set our eyes on our personal agendas, agendas that seek to ensure our power and our goals and to serve our particular communities. We measure successful leadership not by faithfulness to the gospel but by increase in church attendance and budget items. We have lost sight of the source of our renewal—the Holy Spirit. Rest assured that a theology, leadership, a community, a heart, and a faith that are not renewed will die. We must allow God's Spirit to blow where it wills that we may experience God's full and abundant life.

What, then, is the challenge before us? The call of God is that we as a people, as a community of faith, go to Calvary and leave our hopes and dreams, our presuppositions and expectations, our sinfulness and our wounds, our agendas and our battles at the foot of the Cross. We are challenged to face our greatest fear—our loss of control—and allow the Spirit to blow in our midst to give us new visions and new dreams and to set our hearts on fire. We are challenged to be in a constant state of perplexity, but also to be in awe and in abiding astonishment at what God will do in our midst.

To be renewed is to be willing to die. To die is to receive new life. As new men and women, we are called to struggle for the Reign of God. To be part of the Reign is to develop into a new kind of leader: not one who lords, but one who loves; not one who sends, but one who serves; not one who determines, but one who discerns the blowing of the Spirit and responds, "Here I am, Lord. Send me."

## SUGGESTIONS FOR WORSHIP

### Call to Worship

The Spirit and the bride say, "Come."
And let everyone who hears say, "Come."
And let everyone who is thirsty come.
Let anyone who wishes take the water of life as a gift. (Rev. 22:17)

"Come, Lord Jesus!" Come into our midst and make us one.
Come, Lord Jesus, into our midst and make us whole.
Come, Lord Jesus, and make us new.
On this blessed day, let one and all who would be made new, come.

### Prayer of Confession

Dearest Lord, we confess that we have long held our lives and our agendas too precious to leave at the foot of the Cross. We confess that like Jacob at Peniel, we wrestle with you to be in control, even as we proclaim you Lord. We recognize our desire and need to be made new, to be restored, to be brought to wholeness. So we cry out to you, "Come, Lord Jesus!" Let your Spirit blow in our midst, and take away the cobwebs of death and sin that permeate all that we are and all that we have. Come, Lord Jesus! Let your Spirit blow life into the church, into our communities, and into our lives. Make us new in Christ. In Jesus name, we pray. Amen.

## Assurance of Pardon (II Cor. 5:17 adapted)

Whoever is in Christ is a new creation. The old has passed away, behold, the new has come.

## Benediction

We go forth to discover the wonderful adventure of the new life in Christ, challenged to no longer live according to careful formulas for success, but to be blown about by the Spirit. We go forth not as lords, but as servants; not to be served, but to give our life for the Reign of God. May the God who is our Creator, the Son who gave his life as ransom for us, and the Spirit who blows in new life be with us now and always. Shalom.

# Ordinary Time 16 or Proper 11

*Mary G. Graves*

In four-part harmony these texts speak of God's relentless concern to bring the far-off sheep, God's children, back home.

**Jeremiah 23:1-6** speaks judgment on the ineffective shepherd kings of Israel who have basically led the people into exile. Only the personal intervention of God—the Good Shepherd—will bring back the scattered flock. The return from exile is Israel's new deliverance song (instead of the exodus from Egypt), and it is all God's doing, ultimately through the lineage of David, the shepherd king.

**Psalm 23** is both credo and prayer-song about the Good Shepherd ushering each little lamb through the darkness of exile into the mercy and goodness of homecoming. There is an interesting shift of metaphor midway through, from God as shepherd to God as the host at home. It is obvious that dependence on God is what leads us to the promised land and interior rest.

**Ephesians 2:11-22** continues Paul's celebration of the life of the church established through the reconciling work of Jesus Christ, who is its head and its cornerstone. The amazing centerpiece of that reconciling work is the uniting of Jew and Gentile in the household of God—an already accomplished fact that could only be accomplished through the blood of Christ. Only in this Messiah is there the common ground of God's creation bringing these two hopelessly hostile parties together in peace.

**Mark 6:30-34, 53-56** provides the circumference of a passage describing Jesus as the shepherd of Israel. The section begins with Jesus taking the weary disciples, just in from the mission field, off for some rest and relaxation. And it ends with a Marcan summary of the extensive nature of Jesus' compassionate shepherd outreach to all the suffering masses—in villages, cities, and throughout the country.

# REFLECTIONS

Conflict resolution and the healing of family relationships do not spring from peacemaking efforts, political agendas, or extensive therapeutic investments (though each has its own essential place in Christian living). The source of our peace and homecoming is the reconciling work of God accomplished through the death and resurrection of Jesus Christ, the Good Shepherd. He is the hinge that brings the transformation in relationships that cannot come from our own making.

# A SERMON BRIEF

Mark Twain was disturbed at all the discord he saw among God's creatures and so he decided to experiment with the problem. He built a cage, and in it he put a dog and a cat.

"In an hour I taught a cat and a dog to be friends. . . . In another hour I taught them to be friends with a rabbit. In the course of two days I was able to add a fox, a goose, a squirrel, and some doves. Finally a monkey. They lived together in peace, even affectionately.

"Next, in another cage I confined an Irish Catholic from Tipperary, and soon I added a Scotch Presbyterian from Aberdeen. Next a Turk from Constantinople, a Greek Christian from Crete, an Armenian, a Methodist from the wilds of Arkansas, a Buddhist from China, a Brahman from Benares. Finally a Salvation Army Colonel from Wapping. Then I stayed away for two whole days. When I came back to note the results . . . not a specimen [was] left alive."

We have our own experiments, our own examples of intolerance and hopeless division: Bosnian Serbs and Bosnian Muslims lost in bloodshed that defies efforts by the United Nations to stop it; increasing gang violence in U.S. cities with community leaders throwing up their hands in helplessness; rising nationalism in Europe; and tribalism in Africa.

Mark Twain is not the only one disturbed at all the discord he sees among God's creatures. Everywhere we look intolerance and divisiveness are on the rise and seem to be more and more impossible to overcome—even in our homes. We witness complete stalemates between husbands and wives—walls of hurt and hostility between parents and their children; parents divorcing; and brutal custody battles over children—two parties, hopelessly unable to come together even over those things they share in common.

Paul describes something refreshingly different. Here in Ephesians he is writing to Gentiles who have now been welcomed into Christian fellowship with Jews. And he marvels at the miracle of these two very separate groups coming together. Certainly there could be no greater hatred and division anywhere than between Jew and Gentile, a division so deeply embedded that Paul talks about it in a variety of descriptive ways: aliens and citizens, those far off and those near, a dividing wall of hostility.

In their very histories and callings the two groups were very divided. God chose a people, the Jews, to point to God's unique covenant love by being God's covenant partner. And they were marked as such, marked by their behaviors, laws, circumcision, and Temple worship as separate and unique. That's why Paul circles this text with this extreme description of two very separate groups: "you who once were far off" and "those who were near" (Eph. 2:13, 17)—you Gentiles, far removed from even knowing anything about God's covenant love, and then you Jews, the bearers of God's promises all along.

Eventually their different calling turned into vicious name-calling. You've seen the Calvin and Hobbes cartoon when Calvin forms his own club where he is "Stupendous Man" and no girls are allowed because they are yukky and stupid. Likewise Jews and Gentiles degenerated into their own game of name-calling. Gentiles were put down as "dogs" and "pigs," the term "uncircumcision" was loaded with shame and hatred. The Gentiles had their own special contempt of the Jews, seen throughout the pages of scripture in various attempts to kill them off (e.g., Moses at birth).

Yet, you shoot to the end of this passage and you see this miraculous transformation. They are no longer separate, "no longer strangers and aliens," no longer divided, but together, citizens of the same country, living together in the same house! It's like two rival street gangs coming together in the same house.

How in the world could such a hopeless division result in that kind of unity? Only because of the hymn that is found right in the middle of verses 13-18. Everything pivots on the musical number by Jesus that occurs right here. No, Jesus does not have everybody join hands and sing "We Are the World." This is no sentimental pop tune like "Come Together." It is more like Tchaikovsky's *1812* Overture.

I grew up listening to the *1812* Overture. I heard it so much that even though it's not exactly a sing-along number, when I listen to it now I have to sing along. It begins fairly calmly but then escalates into this magnificent battle with cannons firing. And then after intense fighting the battle is done and it bursts into joyous victory music. That is the kind of familiar piece that we have right in the middle of our Ephesians passage, a battle hymn about what Christ has done to bring hopeless divisions, like Gentile and Jew, to an end.

How was that accomplished? "By the blood of Christ" (v. 13), says the familiar church hymn. "In his flesh he has made both groups into one and has broken down the dividing wall, that is, the hostility between us" (v. 14). Christ took care of our divisions personally through his own flesh and blood. Through his death and resurrection the battle has been won. That is the amazing content of Paul's central hymn, "he is our peace;" in his own person he has taken the full frenzy of our hostilities and put it to death. But there are two parts to this battle hymn. Christ personally took care of those hostile forces; he defeated them. But, more than that, Christ has created "in himself one new humanity in place of the two" (v. 15).

Many couples who marry later in life have a tough time deciding whose house they will live in—his or hers? Whose furniture will be used and where? Those are not easy problems to solve when you have lived with these things in your life for a long time. If he moves into her house then it's highly likely that he will always feel like he is on her turf, operating according to her rules—that he never really has equal footing in his own home. And if she moves into his house, the same would be true. I have noticed that it seems to work best when these newlyweds have the opportunity to move into a new house where both are forced to adjust to a new reality and a new way of being together.

That's what Jesus Christ has done. He has created in himself a new reality, a new way of being together that is not dependent on adjusting to old realities. But instead, our differences are transcended, superseded by this new single humanity in Christ, marked by equal access to all. That is the transforming reality that is described in our hymn, this new opportunity bringing Jews and Gentiles together in the church.

The music of Christ invites us to a new reality—beyond our hopeless intolerance and division into a new space where there is universal acceptance and unity. That is what we are called to adjust ourselves to. And more than that, as the church we are called to send out the invitation for all people to come together in God's house as one.

John McCutcheon, a great American folk musician and songwriter, composed a song called "Calling All the Children Home" from the way he remembered his mother calling all the children in for supper when they were growing up. In her musical invitation—"John, Mary Clair, Lulu, Jeanie, Kevin, Jeff, Patty, Nancy, Rob"—he heard God's call.

Home to the table, home to the feast
Where the last are first and the greatest are the least
No one is forgotten, no one is alone
When we're calling all the children home.

That's what the music of Christ's church is all about.

## SUGGESTIONS FOR WORSHIP

### Call to Worship

LEADER: God comes searching for us, seeking our response; like a shepherd, God watches over us.

**PEOPLE: God provides for us all that we need; by still waters, God leads us to green pastures.**

LEADER: God gathers us from many backgrounds and traditions. God rescues us from the shadows of our scattered places.

**PEOPLE: The worship of God restores our souls; the righteousness of God calms our fears.**

LEADER: God lifts us up to the mountain heights; here we are strengthened for life in the valley.

**PEOPLE: Evil and death hold no terror for us; surely God's goodness and mercy will follow us.**

(Lavon Bayler, *Fresh Winds of the Spirit*, book 2 of *Liturgical Resources for Year A* [Cleveland: Pilgrim, 1992] 148.)

### Prayer of Confession

"All we like sheep have gone astray; we have all turned to our own way" (Isa. 53:6). Let us humbly confess our sins before our gracious God:

O God, our Shepherd, we have wandered far from your ways. We have pursued our own ideas as if they were superior to your truth. We live with secrets that we fear to be known. We are afraid to face evil, to confront those we label enemies, to deal with issues of life and death. We are sometimes rigid and legalistic. We blame others for our own failures. Turn us around so we can accept your forgiveness, live more positively in the future, and truly rejoice in your good news. Amen (Bayler, 60).

## Assurance of Pardon

Jesus said, "I am the good shepherd. I know my own and my own know me, . . . I lay down my life for the sheep" (John 10:14-15). This is the good news that is ours through the death and resurrection of Jesus Christ—by his stripes we are healed. Thanks be to God!

## Benediction

May God's goodness and mercy follow you all the days of your life; and may you dwell in the household of God forever. Amen.

# Ordinary Time 17 or Proper 12

## Mary G. Graves

In all four texts there is the Bread of Heaven meeting us beyond our wildest expectations at the very center of our need.

**II Kings 4:42-44** comes at the end of the miracles of the prophet Elisha. This particular cameo miracle involves one hundred hungry people, a too-small amount of food, and the word of the Lord saying, "They shall eat and have some left." Sure enough, they had more than enough to eat and some left over "according to the word of the LORD" (v. 45).

**Psalm 145:10-18** is a well-worn communal prayer of praise, highly structured (an "alphabet psalm") in spelling out God's tangible ways of being gracious and faithful to all—"all your works," "all people," "all who are falling," "all who are bowed down," "You . . . (satisfy) the desire of every living thing."

**Ephesians 3:14-21** is another big prayer (the first was in chapter 1) offered to a great God on behalf of these Ephesian believers by their spiritual father, Paul. The prayer is for an experiential knowing—a heart knowledge of God. It is also a paradoxical knowing because the fullness and love of God is beyond knowing. Yet believers have an indwelling Messiah, who comes from outside our knowing (believers are recipients—"rooted and grounded . . . filled") to dwell "in your inner being . . . in your hearts."

**John 6:1-21** is the first third of a chapter that could be titled "The Bread Discourse"—the theme being the bread that Jesus gives his disciples to eat. The bread is for a multitude of five thousand—once again, not near enough bread ("what are they among so many people?"). Yet the twelve basketfuls left over made clear that Jesus was an unusual prophet-king resource. This is reinforced by the narrative immediately following describing Jesus walking on the sea and speaking to the disciples' terror: "It is I; do not be afraid."

## REFLECTIONS

Praying to this God who "is able to accomplish abundantly far more than all we can ask or imagine" (Eph. 3:20) is the priority here—through the prophet Elisha, through the psalmist, through Jesus, through Paul. It is a relational connection that precedes a rational connection. The invitation is compelling—to have our deepest heart-felt needs met by the transcendent God of covenant love who meets us in the flesh in Jesus Christ. The invitation is also one of paradox; it is not manageable or understandable, but a mysterious invitation "to know the love of Christ that surpasses knowledge" (Eph. 3:19). There's a wonderful mix of God's transcendence and immanence here, a balance that needs to be named and protected in our preaching.

## A SERMON BRIEF

I talked recently with a new mother in this church the day after her son was born and said, "Congratulations! How did it go?"

She said, "Well, the first four hours of labor were unbearable until they gave me an epidural, and then it was a piece of cake."

I've never had a baby so I could only know intellectually what she was saying. But you who have given birth know experientially why an epidural seems like the greatest gift of God on earth. There's a difference between knowing something intellectually and knowing something experientially.

There's a difference between knowing something because you've heard about it and knowing something because you've actually lived it. Paul is praying here for the readers to know God. Both of his prayers are about the knowledge of God. But, you will notice that it is not a knowledge about God for which he is praying but a direct, firsthand, internalized experience of God. There is a big difference.

I met a delightful man, an elder in a Presbyterian church in the midwest, just retired as a university professor, investing even more time in the church. We were in a small group forum where we each shared our journey of faith, and he said, "I grew up in a Presbyterian church. When I moved out of the house I got married in another Presbyterian church, got involved there, and served as an elder. Then I was invited to a Christian businessmen's association and flew to one of their conferences. This conference made a huge impact on me. These guys acted like God was really alive. They prayed for me and I entered into a whole new experience of God in my life."

It is possible to know all about God, up here (in the head), even among those of us in the church without knowing and experiencing God directly, firsthand, interacting with God "like God was really alive."

Paul is praying for his readers to have a heart-knowledge of the living God, that "the eyes of your heart [be] enlightened" (Eph. 1:18). He's praying that his readers experience God directly, concretely, that they enter into a real and deeply internalized knowledge of God's love and power. They can't get it secondhand from Paul; they need to experience God themselves.

Yet Paul's prayer presents a paradox. "I pray that you may . . . know the love of Christ that surpasses knowledge" (Eph. 3:19-20). He prays that his readers might know God personally, but he also admits that this God is beyond any person's capacity to know. He names these two opposite truths side by side on purpose, because the God that we are invited to know is both a transcendent and immanent God.

God is transcendent, too holy and great to fathom, but also God has come to us personally in Jesus Christ, "God-with-us" and is near and available, as near and available as the air we breathe.

Neither end of that spectrum—the transcendent or the immanent—can be neglected in our knowledge of God.

The transcendent end of the spectrum is what was felt when the moon landing was made twenty-eight years ago and the astronauts looked back upon their view of earth and exclaimed, "There is a God!" The immanent end of the spectrum is what is felt when you hear the music of "Amazing Grace" on bagpipes and all of a sudden tears well up within you. We are called to that full spectrum, to a firsthand knowing of the fullness of God, a God whom Paul describes to us as completely transcendent and completely immanent, and with Paul we must not collapse either end of that spectrum or else we are no longer relating to God.

We are so tempted to do that—to make God more manageable by somehow undoing this paradox—making God less holy on the one end or making God less accessible on the other. Paul doesn't do that. Instead he prays within the paradox, that we would be filled and encountered by the fullness of God.

God's transcendence is mind-boggling, immeasurable, and beyond description. There's a Tibetan story about two frogs. One lived by the sea and the other lived in a deep well. One day the frog from the sea decided to go and visit the frog who lived in the well. During this visit the well frog asked the sea frog, "How big is the sea? Is it half as big as my well?" The sea frog said, "Oh, no! It is far bigger than that." The well frog said, "Is it twice as big as my well?" The sea frog responded, "The only way for you to know the size of the sea is to come and to see it for yourself." So, the frog from the well traveled with the sea frog toward the sea and when they got to the top of the last hill the sea frog told him to close his eyes while he led him the last steps to the top. When the well frog opened his eyes and looked out at the sea his mind exploded into a thousand pieces.

The vastness of God is too big for us to handle. It explodes any of our thoughts of who God is. That is why Karl Barth referred to God as Wholly Other, the God who is completely beyond us and comes from outside us. Karl Barth was criticized for overemphasizing the transcendence of God. Many felt that he was so successful in naming God's otherness that it left us with a God who was too far away, too removed, too inaccessible to be known in a personal way.

For too long many mainline churches have protected God's transcendence to the neglect of God's immanence. We have been great at singing with the angels: "Holy, Holy, Holy, Lord God Almighty!," but we are not so great at singing with the psalmist: O God, you are my God, earnestly I seek you; my soul thirsts for you, in a dry and weary land where there is no water.

We just aren't very good at talking about God in a firsthand, relational way. I believe this neglect is at least partially responsible for the great rise in what is called the New Age Movement with its emphasis on a personal experience of God.

James Redfield, in his book *The Celestine Prophecy*, has catapulted New Age thinking to the top of the *New York Times* best-seller list for months. Alan Atkisson comments in his book review, "Hundreds of thousands of American book buyers, many of whom would never set foot inside a metaphysical book-and-crystal store, are snapping it up, giving it away, staying up all night to finish reading it, talking about it with their friends, even studying it in their church groups" (Alan Atkisson, review of *The Celestine Prophecy,* by James Redfield, "The New Age Journal" [July 1994]: 60).

Why are people so hungry for this book? Perhaps it is the same reason Redfield was hungry to write it. James Redfield grew up attending a little country Methodist church with his mother, but he always felt there was something missing. In his words, "There were revivals and such, and people would have conversion experiences, but there wasn't any dialogue about the spiritual experience itself. If you asked people about it, they'd talk about . . . community love for one another, but not about what it really felt like to be touched by the spirit" (Atkisson, 60).

Are we able to talk about what it means to experience God firsthand? Are we able to dialogue with one another about those ways we experience God's presence in our lives, what it really feels like to be touched by the Holy Spirit?

Could it be that we need to develop and expand our syntax when it comes to communicating about the activity of God in our lives?

Paul is not at all shy about talking about his own spiritual experiences with a very immanent God. He thought of God's nearness in terms of union with Christ, being "in Christ," and "Christ in me."

That is why he prays the way he does, that we would be strengthened in our inner being, that Christ take up permanent residence at the center of our personalities, that we be filled with all the fullness of God, that we receive God's Spirit of wisdom and revelation opening the very eyes of our hearts. The God who is beyond me meets me right where I am, at the center of who I am. I can actually know and experience this loving God whose love surpasses knowledge.

It is possible though to so emphasize God's immanence, God's presence with us, that God's transcendence is sacrificed. That is the major deficit of New Age thinking. New Age spirituality encourages an inner consciousness of our unity with God. In fact, God is seen as so immanent that "my self is God." God's transcendent otherness totally disappears. God is so merged with who I am that I am empowered to achieve my own salvation. The ninth insight in *The Celestine Prophecy* claims that humans can so connect to God's source of energy that their own energy levels increase. They become as God. In such an increased state of vibration, humans will be able to walk straight into heaven.

Paul talked about his spiritual experiences with God but he never said, "I am God, God is me." Contrary to New Age thinking, we cannot become God. God is Wholly Other. We can experience God's love intimately and completely but only as it comes to us from one who is outside ourselves. That is why Paul talks about being rooted and grounded, being filled and enlightened. You look at the tenses of those verbs and you can see that we are passive recipients of an action of God that happens to us; the source of this relationship of power and love is in God, not us.

So, enough talking about the full spectrum of God. How can you and I be filled with the fullness of God? How can we experience firsthand this intimate knowing that Paul is praying about?

The first step is simple: It is to say "Yes" to God's generous offer to make a loving home in your heart and to invite Christ to take up permanent residence there. Once you have yielded yourself to God you don't need to second-guess whether Jesus is with you or not; even when you don't feel like it, Jesus is there.

The ongoing challenge, however, is learning how to pay attention to this inner life of the Spirit. This is a lifelong challenge and cannot be done alone. You and I must have constant clarification from others through Christ's church—worshiping together, listening and speaking God's Word together, and most of all having other companions on the road of faith who can help us be aware of the activity of God in our lives—and then figure out how best to respond.

# SUGGESTIONS FOR WORSHIP

## Call to Worship (Ps. 145:10, 13*b*-16, 18)

LEADER: All your works shall give thanks to you, O LORD, and all your faithful shall bless you.

PEOPLE: **The LORD is faithful in all his words, and gracious in all his deeds.**

LEADER: The LORD upholds all who are falling, and raises up all who are bowed down.

PEOPLE: **The eyes of all look to you, and you give them their food in due season.**

LEADER: You open your hand, satisfying the desire of every living thing.

PEOPLE: **The LORD is near to all who call on him, to all who call on him in truth.**

## Prayer of Confession (Mark 8:17-21)

The disciples were fussing about having no bread. Jesus questioned them: "Why are you talking about having no bread? Do you still not perceive or understand?

"Are your hearts hardened?

"Do you have eyes, and fail to see?

"Do you have ears, and fail to hear?

"And do you not remember? When I broke the five loaves for the five thousand, how many baskets full of broken pieces did you collect?"

They said to him, "Twelve."

"And the seven for the four thousand, how many baskets full of broken pieces did you collect?"

And they said to him, "Seven."

Then he said to them, "Do you not yet understand?"

In this time of silent confession let Jesus ask you about your own dullness toward all that God is doing in and around you.

(Silent prayer.)

## Assurance of Pardon

"A new heart I will give you, and a new spirit I will put within you; and I will remove from your body the heart of stone and give you a heart of flesh. I will put my spirit within you, and make you follow my statutes and be careful to observe my ordinances. Then you shall live in the land that I gave to your ancestors; and you shall be my people, and I will be your God. I will save you from all your uncleannesses, and I will summon the grain and make it abundant and lay no famine upon you" (Ezek. 36:26-29).

In the name of Jesus Christ, the Bread of Heaven, you are a forgiven people! Thanks be to God!

## Benediction (based on Eph. 3:20-21)

> Now to the God, who by the power at work within us
> is able to accomplish abundantly far more
> than all we can ask or imagine,
> To this God be glory in the church
> and in Christ Jesus to all generations,
> forever and ever. Amen.

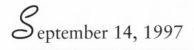

# Ordinary Time 24 or Proper 19

*Alyce M. McKenzie*

**Proverbs 1:20-33:** Wisdom cries aloud in the street.

**Psalm 19:** The heavens are telling the glory of God.

**James 3:1-12:** The tongue is a dangerous organ.

**Mark 8:27-38:** Those who follow Christ must be willing to face suffering, rejection, and death.

## REFLECTIONS

According to Claudia Camp, the figure of Woman Wisdom is the product of the postexilic era and is informed by the social images and roles of women in that time: home-schooling wisdom teachers, managers of households, and wifely counselors and lovers. Women's roles came to the forefront as the locus of wisdom activity shifted from places of public stir to the arena of the home.

Woman Wisdom was also informed by images and roles of women from the biblical witness. One such image was of the woman who ventured from the private into the public domain in search of justice. Woman Wisdom standing at the city gates may well draw on the memory of Tamar (Genesis 38) and Ruth as seekers of justice. These women, while denied their rightful position by circumstance and injustice at the city gates, regain it and, in the process, serve God's ends. The city gates were the place of legal judgment, which often took the form of male decisions on the actions of women. In the two stories recorded in today's texts, women come to the place of judgment to judge the judges, to point up the failures of current systems of justice and inspire changes in them that will meet the needs of the vulnerable more equitably (Claudia V. Camp, *Wisdom and the Feminine in the Book of Proverbs* [Sheffield, England: JSOT Press, 1985], 126-33).

The recovery of this aspect of Woman Wisdom's identity empowers women to raise their voices on behalf of society's vulnerable. For Woman Wisdom boldly comes to the city gates to judge the judges for their failure to choose her counsel (*'esa*) and reproof (*tokahat*) one too many times. Her teachings are embodied in the sayings of Proverbs chapters 10–31. She stresses the life or death choice of the path of wisdom over the path of folly. Reverence for God and others, graciousness to the poor, moderation, and industry pave the path of wisdom beneath one's feet. This path leads to that personal and social shalom, that orderly existence that the sages tended to equate with life (Prov. 3:18; 8:35-36). Opposite choices pave the path of folly, which leads to disorder and calamity, both personal and communal.

Like Woman Wisdom, Jesus offers counsel, but his is a subversive brand of wisdom, challenging human wisdom's equation of life with safety and comfort. Like her, he reproves both Peter and others, challenging them to fear what they have always wanted and to choose what they have always feared.

## A Sermon Brief

Wisdom is personified as a woman in the book of Proverbs, primarily in chapters 2–9. The sages after the exile used the literary device of personification to clarify very abstract attributes of God. Thus by appealing in almost hymnic language in Proverbs 8:22-36, Wisdom esteems herself as a woman who is brought forth as the very first act of the Lord's creation. Rather than presenting herself as an alternative divine being, Woman Wisdom emerges in this period after the exile, as an expression of the gift of God's guidance in the midst of daily human life. Early Christians saw deep connections between wisdom and Jesus, which emerge in many places in Paul's writings, and in the Gospels. One such common trait between them is where they take their stand. They both take their stand to teach in the thick of things. Woman Wisdom physically places herself in the street, on the square, at the busiest corner, at the city gate. Jesus, in this passage from Mark's Gospel, takes his stand on the well-traveled roads of Galilee, and in other scenes we find him in the Temple, in the homes of religious leaders, setting his face toward Jerusalem. Divine Wisdom wants to be where there are lots of people, where there is lots of noise, lots of confusion, where human transactions of all kinds—social, economic, political, legal, and emotional—are going on, where there is bound to be conflict. That means public places, streets like Hope Street in Philadelphia where you can't walk your dog for fear of syringe needles poking its paws, or Logavina Street in Sarajevo, where you can't walk to get water without being hit by a sniper's shot.

That means private places as well, where domestic abuse is the number one cause of emergency room visits by women and every day four women are murdered by husbands or boyfriends (*Daughters of Sarah*, [summer 1994], 9).

Zlata Filipovic is a young Bosnian girl growing up in Sarajevo who began keeping a diary in September 1991, a few months before Serbian artillery positions were set up on the hills directly above her house. Her family had to move into the front room, piling sandbags against the windows to protect them from shrapnel, then to the cellar. Her best friends were killed playing in the local park. Supplies ran low and then ran out. Electricity and water stopped flowing. Because the Serbs often targeted schools and playgrounds, school was stopped. Zlata was not allowed to go outside and play, so she had to stay in the apartment. Whenever it seemed safe, she would practice the piano, which was in her parents' bedroom—one of the more dangerous rooms. She played Bach and Chopin even while the sound of machine guns echoed from the hills. It gave her comfort to know that, despite the war, her playing was improving. For a short while, it also made her forget that outside in the streets below her, a war was being fought (Zlata Filipovic, *Zlata's Diary: A Child's Life in Sarajevo* [New York: Scholastic, 1994], vii-viii). In the midst of the war-torn places of life, Wisdom positions herself, beckoning to us like the draw of beautiful music to Zlata, sometimes disturbing, sometimes soothing.

To say that Wisdom takes her stand in the thick of things is to make a statement about where she places herself in the spiritual geography of our inward lives: in the most confused, conflicted intersections. The apocryphal book The Wisdom of Solomon expresses this poetically: "One who rises early to seek her will have no difficulty, for she will be found sitting at the gate" (6:14). Stretching out her hand to us, as we trudge along well-worn paths that are leading us nowhere we want to go, she is crying out her urgent refrain, "How long? How long?"

Jesus, too, takes his stand in the thick of things, where there are bound to be crowds and conflict, in the outer and the inward worlds. Like her, his wisdom calls to us as we walk along pleasant paths that lead to death, calling us to life. The Gospels highlight the fact that people often felt more conflicted after they had encountered Jesus than they had before. For his wisdom is not designed to help us maintain a surface order in our lives, but to challenge the false orders we have created. This means that the places we thought we had walled off, that we hoped had been smoothed over, are disturbed and churning, now that we've met Jesus. That feels like bad news, but it's on the way to being good news.

In this passage from Mark, we observe Jesus' teachings arousing discomfort in his disciples. Teachings like "The Son of Man must undergo great suffering, and be rejected by the elders, the chief priests, and the scribes, and be killed, and after three days rise again" (8:31). "Get behind me, Satan! For you are setting your mind not on divine things but on human things" (8:33).

"Those who want to save their life will lose it, and those who lose their life for my sake, and for the sake of the gospel, will save it" (8:35).

Divine Wisdom, as personified in Woman Wisdom and as embodied in Jesus, goes out into the thick of human life, crying out, stretching out a hand, challenging hearers to accept God's teachings before it is too late. In situations of domestic abuse, Wisdom stretches out a hand to women, crying out, "If you truly want to help him, you will have to leave him." God extends wisdom to the abuser as well as the abused. In Oak Park, Illinois, a program for men who abuse women tries to educate men in new ways of dealing with anger and frustration. A gang member, who had entered the eighteen-week program with a very macho idea of what it means to be a man, had these words to say as he graduated: "Now I know I don't have to hurt another person to be a man" ("Women and Violence," *Daughters of Sarah*, summer 1994, 3). Divine Wisdom is extended like an outstretched hand to all those places where people, ourselves included, realize that things can't keep going along this path—whether it is the need for a church to find new leadership in the midst of a painful division, or for a substance abuser to seek treatment, or for a community to address teen violence.

Woman Wisdom and Jesus summon us as a community of faith to come and stand with her and him in all those places, too. Woman Wisdom and Jesus summon us like John Wesley, who left the safe sanctuaries of the Church of England and went and preached to men and women in the fields. He went and stood by the path leading out of the mines. He stood, preaching the good news as the miners, some of them young boys, crawled out of the filthy pits and wound their way home to their tuppence buckets of gin. The good news stands on those corners, at those gates, in those places where it is needed most.

On what corner in this community is Wisdom standing, calling us to come and take our stand with her? At what confused crossroads is Jesus standing, stretching out his hand, calling "How long?"

## Suggestions for Worship

### Call to Worship (based on Psalm 19)

LEADER: Wisdom cries out in the street; in the squares she raises her voice.

PEOPLE: **As Jesus taught along the most crowded roads of Galilee, so today the Risen Christ cries out to us on the busiest corners of life.**

LEADER: At the entrance of today's city gates, God's Wisdom speaks, inviting us to accept so precious a divine gift.

PEOPLE:     May our hearts rejoice this day in the precepts of the Lord.

LEADER:     May our eyes be enlightened by the commandment of God.

PEOPLE:     May we desire the ordinances of the Lord more than fine gold and the drippings of the honeycomb.

ALL:        May all our thoughts, words, and actions spring from the pure well of the fear of the Lord.

## Prayer of Confession

We ask your forgiveness for those times we have stayed on the outskirts of a controversy we should have been in the middle of, because we were too busy, or cowardly, or in the mood to tell people what they wanted to hear. Forgive us for the times we have ignored the sound of the still small voice of wisdom in the thick of conflicts within and without, because we have been so enamored with the sound of our own voice. Forgive us for our efforts to transform Jesus into our own image, as one who sought comfort and security, and help us risk allowing him to be who he will be in and through our lives.

## Assurance of Pardon

Scripture assures us that those who answer Wisdom's call will have no dread of disaster. Whoever loses their life for Jesus' sake and for the sake of the gospel will find it. We are called and empowered to lose paralyzing guilt and self-loathing in the gracious embrace of Christ, so that we might find ourselves loving self and others in a freer, clearer way, even as God has first loved us.

## Benediction

Go forth to walk in the path of Wisdom, no longer confusing material security and the elimination of risk with life. As you daily rise to the challenge of the teachings of Jesus Christ, may you know the courage and peace that come from placing our trust in the Wisdom that God imparts to us through God's Presence.

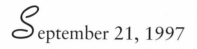

# Ordinary Time 25 or Proper 20

## *Alyce M. McKenzie*

**Proverbs 31:10-31:** A worthy woman is more precious than jewels.

**Psalm 1:** Blessed is the one who walks not in the counsel of the wicked.

**James 3:13–4:3, 7-8a:** The wisdom from above is pure.

**Mark 9:30-37:** Whoever would be first, must be last of all.

## REFLECTIONS

Recent scholarship asserts that "A Poem to a Woman of Worth," *'esel hayil* (literally, a "woman of strength"), depicts not a role model for women's daily accomplishments, but Woman Wisdom herself (Thomas P. McCreesh, O.P. "Wisdom as Wife: Proverbs 31:10-31," in *Revue Biblique,* [Paris: École Practique D'Etudes Bibliques Etablié au couvent Dominicain St. Etienne de Jerusalem, 1985], 25-46). It is placed at the end of the book, organized as an alphabetical acrostic, a hymn of praise to the attributes and benefits of Woman Wisdom (McCreesh, 25-26).

While this depiction of Wisdom is not meant as a model for daily accomplishment for actual women, then or now, it is informed by the skills and admirable qualities of postexilic Hebrew women. Woman Wisdom is not simply the maintainer of a household, but the source of its identity. This mirrors the role of women in postexilic Israelite society. With the collapse of the male-dominated, mediating institutions of temple and court, and the eclipse of the public influence of king and priest, the home became the focus of community life. There the activities of women, both in running the household and in teaching wisdom to the young, became crucial for the very survival of the community.

Woman Wisdom, while challenging the patriarchal context out of which she arose, is also shaped and bridled by it. In Proverbs her guidance is directed only to young men. She images foolishness and community chaos in terms of sexual union with foreign women. She utters some misogynist proverbs, and before long, in the Wisdom of Jesus Ben Sirach, Woman Wisdom is formally equated with Torah, taught to and read almost exclusively by males (*Wisdom and the Feminine in the Book of Proverbs* [Detroit: Almond Press, 1985). On the positive side, she does represent an honoring of the skills and contributions of women as purveyors of wisdom, then and now. Many of her proverbs acknowledge that human wisdom is limited (19:21) and that God retains the freedom to subvert oppressive systems of so-called wisdom that silence marginal groups.

Jesus taught in proverbs and aphorisms, subverting some of traditional wisdom's concern for personal and social order with behaviors that challenged the social, political, and religious status quo. Some early communities began to envision him, first as Wisdom's envoy, then as Wisdom come to earth. Recovering the theological and biblical connections between Wisdom and Jesus reveals how deep is the debt of each to the other. She represents an honoring of daily experience as the realm of God's care and a recognition of the limitations of human systems of knowledge. He takes up the subversive implications of her wisdom, speaking in proverbs that challenge what passed for wisdom in his day.

# A SERMON BRIEF

This last portion of Proverbs is often called "A Poem to a Woman of Worth." Her hands are always busy, never still, seeking wool and flax, bringing food, planting a vineyard, spinning cloth, helping the needy, sewing garments for her household, doing all the tasks Israelite women had done for centuries. Today, some of the tasks have changed, and they now include tasks outside the home as well as those within it. Still the hands of women, like this woman, are busy performing the tasks that fulfill the crucial function of maintaining home and community.

Who is this woman? There is an uncanny similarity between the qualities of this woman of worth and Woman Wisdom we have encountered in the first thirty chapters of Proverbs. Both are said to shed light on the way of those who follow them (compare 31:18*b* with 13:9); and both are said to be worth more than precious jewels (compare 31:10*b* with 3:15, 8:11, 16:16, 18:19, and 21:15). Both bring prosperity, protection, and honor upon those who trust in them (compare 4:6, 8, 9 with 31:11, 12). Both Woman Wisdom and this woman of worth laugh at the future, the former at the calamity that overtakes those who choose against her (1:26), the latter because of the security that comes to those who choose her (31:25). An especially telling similarity is the mention of the "fear of the LORD." Throughout the Proverbs, we have been repeatedly told that the fear of the Lord, reverence for God as the wellspring of moral knowledge, is the beginning of wisdom (1:7, 9:10, 15:33). The woman of worth, in the concluding verses of Proverbs, is described as "a woman who fears the LORD."

Their uncanny resemblance is no coincidence! This woman of worth is Woman Wisdom herself! This poem comes at the very end of Proverbs to sum up all the qualities of Wisdom and to commend all her benefits to potential followers. It is an invitation to become members of her household and there discover that God both honors us for what is past and strengthens our hands for the work before us.

Columnist and novelist Anna Quindlen, in an interview on "The Charlie Rose Show" broadcast in December 1994, fondly recalls the unconditional love her mother showed her and her brothers and sisters. "With my mother, you didn't have to tap dance, or win prizes to earn her love. She just thought that we were the most marvelous beings that ever dropped onto the face of the earth. My mother was the one true thing in my life—the foundation, the bedrock, that which could be trusted." When Anna was nineteen years old, her mother died and she had to come home from college to help raise her younger siblings, writing excuse notes to school when they were sick, packing lunches, ironing, and mopping.

She went on to become a Pulitzer prize-winning columnist for the *New York Times*, but she recently left her prestigious job there to write novels full-time. Her first novel, filled with autobiographical poignancy, is about a young journalist named Ellen who, at her father's insistence, quits her job and comes home to care for her mother, Kate, who has been diagnosed with cancer. Kate is a woman whose hands Ellen has watched for years, constantly busy bathing children, rocking them, pulling them in wagons, making lunches, cooking, wallpapering, stenciling, and generally making the house a home for Ellen and her brothers and her father, a self-centered English professor. Her mother's hands were ceaselessly working to bring honor, order, and ease to Ellen and her father and brothers.

Ellen has always slightly scorned her mother for not going to college and for being a full-time homemaker. Her mother was like the dinner her hands prepared every night. You needed it for nourishment, but you never thought much about what went into it. Ellen had never thought about the fact that her mother's loving, forgiving acceptance of everyone in the family gave the household its identity, and had given her the strength to pursue her own dreams. Taking over her mother's role, Ellen began to live her way into all her mother had given up and all that her mother had accomplished.

In the months she spent with her dying mother, her mother's hands, no longer able to be ceaselessly useful for others, were free for both sorrow and for joy: for sorrow, as she lamented to Ellen the opportunities she had not been able to pursue, the influence she could have had; for joy, as her hands now were free to hold the novels she had loved as a young woman. Ellen shook her head in amazement at her mother's intelligence and insight, as her hands now became the ones busy preparing the meals and bathing her mother's shrinking body. And while she saw that she could never and would never choose to repeat her mother's life story, she began, increasingly, to honor her mother in the privacy of her own thoughts. Anna Quindlen named her novel about Ellen and Kate in tribute to her own mother, *One True Thing* (New York: Random House, 1994).

"Give her a share in the fruit of her hands, and let her works praise her in the city gates" (Prov. 31:31).

Let us say these words to the mothers, grandmothers, sisters, aunts, friends, foremothers in faith, whose hands worked ceaselessly to bring honor to others, honor to us. Their hands paved the way for women today to make our way to the city gates to take up places of honor and to challenge systems that dishonor others.

Let us allow Jesus to say these words to Woman Wisdom, for he well knew the works of her hands in honoring others and God. Our passage from Mark portrays Jesus' hands gesturing as he teaches his disciples about servant leadership, beckoning children to come to him, and embracing the child as a beloved member of the household of wisdom.

So his invitation echoes hers, to become members of a gracious household. When we accept it, we are empowered to become champions of children and others on the margins. Our hands become busy with his works, and, looking down at our own hands, we are reminded of her who has taught us both. We take a moment to "give (a Wise Woman) a share in the fruit of her hands, and to let her works (mirrored in our works) praise her in the city gates."

## Suggestions for Worship

### Call to Worship

LEADER: The way of Wisdom is like the light of dawn, which shines brighter and brighter until full day.

PEOPLE: **She is more precious than jewels, and nothing you desire can compare with her.**

LEADER: Get wisdom; get insight; do not forget, nor turn away from the words of her mouth.

PEOPLE: **Do not forsake her, and she will keep you.**

LEADER: Love her, and she will guard you.

ALL: **Prize her highly and she will exalt you; she will honor you if you embrace her. She will place on your head a fair garland; she will bestow on you a beautiful crown.**

## Prayer of Confession

We ask forgiveness for the ways in which we have evaded our responsibility to use our strength and wisdom to guide and empower the hands of others for service. We ask forgiveness for the times when, out of our own insecurities, we have denigrated the wisdom of others. Strengthen us to live your Way of servant leadership, to invite those on the margins into the household of Wisdom and to go forth from that household with Your nourishment and warming light to all the world.

## Assurance of Pardon

Members of the Household of Faith, be assured that in our search for forgiveness, God has drawn near to us in Jesus Christ. For the rest of our earthly days and into eternity, we are encircled by the loving arms of Christ, who sheds light on our path and fills our souls with the nourishment of wisdom.

## Benediction (based on Ps. 1:1-3)

Blessed are those who walk not in the counsel of the wicked, nor stand in the way of sinners, nor sit in the seat of scoffers—but whose delight is in God's law. For you shall be like trees planted by streams of water, that brings forth fruit in season, whose leaf does not wither. In all that you do shall you prosper.

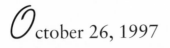

# Ordinary Time 30 or Proper 25

## *Loida Martell-Otero*

**Job 42:1-6, 10-17:** Job repents and is restored.

**Psalm 34:1-8:** God delivers the afflicted.

**Hebrews 7:23-28:** Christ is the perfect high priest.

**Mark 10:46-52:** Jesus heals Bartimaeus.

### REFLECTIONS

If being blind is difficult and frustrating nowadays, even with all our modern technology and the sensitivity we purport to have, imagine how much more terrible and inhumane it must have been in Jesus' time. In that culture, being blind was understood to be a punishment of God for some sin, either by the blind person or his or her family. Therefore, to be blind was to be abandoned by the community of faith, who is supposed to protect the afflicted. To be blind was to be ritually impure. To be blind was to be taken out of that community of faith, which was akin to saying, "God has abandoned you." It also implied that one was deprived of the economic, political, and social means of that day. Thus, to be blind meant that one was poor. A blind person was a "nonperson."

It is not surprising, therefore, that the majority of the blind presented in the Gospel stories are beggars and have no names. Even the blind man in Mark 10:46-52 has no name of his own, being referred to by his genealogy. We only know him as *Bar*, which means "son of," and *Timaeus*, that is, "impure." Maybe he came from one of those unfortunate families, filled with tragedies, similar to the ones we have known—families caught in a net of pain: alcoholism, drugs, abuse, poverty, unemployment, homelessness. Thus, we know this blind man, not by his name but by his story of being rejected by the community: Bartimaeus.

# A Sermon Brief

The story in Mark 10:46-52 begins with Bartimaeus in the street. It was not an unusual scene: a blind beggar in the street. No one paid him any mind. There were so many like him. Bartimaeus was not extraordinary. What was extraordinary were the unfolding events taking place. The famous pilgrimage of pious Jews to Jerusalem to celebrate the Passover had begun. Jericho was a way station on the road. People came out of their homes to encourage and wish the pilgrims well. They were good people, good-hearted, religious . . . and blind. They could see those who were like them: good folk, decent folk, religious pilgrims. But they were incapable of seeing those outside of their circle: "bad" people, the "bums," the beggars, the "socially impure." The sad thing is, this goes on today. Nelson Mandela once commented that he did not fear evil people; rather he feared good people who kept silent in the face of evil.

All these people ignored Bartimaeus, one more beggar, one more nonhuman. All except one: Jesus. Jesus was going by that day, on his way to Jerusalem, on his way to celebrate his last Passover. He knew his days were numbered. Yet, the weight of this reality did not make him deaf to the cries of Bartimaeus. His sadness and pain did not make him insensitive to the pain of Bartimaeus. On the contrary, Jesus knew that cry well. God-made-human, Jesus came to save all who cry from pain. Jesus had come for Bartimaeus.

Jesus' ministry incarnated the good news, "God reigns!" "God reigns" gave notice to the principalities and powers. "God reigns" gave notice to death and sin. "God reigns" gave notice to all that distorts the purpose of God for our lives, personal and social. To all that is oppressive, to all that is evil, to all that is satanic: *God* reigns. God is in charge. In Jesus the Reign of God was near, especially for those who had suffered, who had been victims of oppression and abuse. In Christ Jesus, God had intervened in human history to rescue the forgotten, the rejected, the thrown away, the ones rendered nonhuman.

Jesus knew, however, that his ministry could not just be proclamation. His calling involved action. Jesus knew that the only way to liberate the captives was by paying the price for their ransom. Thus, Jesus was on the way to Jerusalem to celebrate his last Passover and to die on the Cross—to die for me, for you, for the Bartimaeuses of life, to slay death, so that God could reign in our lives. For God to reign in our lives, Jesus had to embody, in his living and dying, the implications of this good news. He had to stop before the cry of Bartimaeus.

The people were bothered by Bartimaeus's insistent cry. You know, there are times in which challenges are insistent, and we get bothered. We want to live a comfortable gospel, without too much bother. Business as usual. However, to live the good news implies living under constant challenges, uncomfortable changes, and insistent calls from God. Jesus was not bothered by the cry. He did not say, "Oh what a bother! And with all the important things I have on my agenda. . . . " No. Jesus stopped. He stopped for this beggar, for this impure one. He stopped for Bartimaeus because he had good news for Bartimaeus. And so Jesus called out to him. Bartimaeus was not "one more thing" to be passed by. He was a human being, deserving of attention. How wonderful to know that we have a Christ who does not pass us by ignoring our cries and tears! He does not say that he has more important things to do. He stops.

Bartimaeus, on the other hand, did not hesitate in responding to Jesus' call. He threw aside his mantle. He threw aside his cover, his protection, his bed, his shelter. He threw it aside immediately, and he presented himself before Jesus. Sometimes, the problem with our Christian lives is that we ask God to intervene, but we want it to be done smoothly, gently. "Don't rock the boat, Jesus! Help me, but don't get into my life. Don't take off the mantle." We all have mantles that we need to throw aside in order to experience Christ's transforming power. We must throw aside the mantles that cover us, protect us, hide us and bind us. Bartimaeus threw aside his mantle, and presented himself to Jesus, no longer a thing, but a person. Jesus looked at him. I can imagine the look of love, of tenderness, of understanding. How wonderful to know that in the midst of our tragedies there is One who says, "I understand."

Then Jesus asked him, "What do you want?" What a foolish question! Is it not obvious what this man wants? Why ask? Sometimes we say, "Why should I pray for this or that? God knows my heart and my needs." God requires that we ask because God respects us. God does not assume. God does not barge into our hearts or our lives. Therefore, Jesus asked the question. He recognized the human dignity of this man. Sometimes we fail in our attempts to help the fallen and the needy. Then we seek something or someone to blame. Frustrated, we give up. We do not realize that often the problem is that we have sought the answers *without asking what the problem is.*

Bartimaeus's answer was quick: "Let me see again." And Jesus was just as quick to respond: "Go; your faith has made you well." A word of healing. A word of restoration. A word of hope. A word of liberation. A word of salvation. Why? Because from being a nobody, ritually impure, Bartimaeus became a human being. He knew that God had not abandoned him. From being prostrate on the street, he now stood on his two feet. From being blind, he could see. He became somebody. And he followed Jesus.

What are we now to do before this passage? Jesus died for the nobodies, the rejected, the forgotten that we are unable to see. God reigns! At the Cross, he slew alcoholism, drug addiction, greed, abuse, abandonment, indifference, racism—all the things that oppose God's Reign. And Jesus rose on the third day to bring new life, transformed life, abundant life, eternal life—life that invites us to throw aside our mantles of comfortableness and protection. We are invited to risk living the good news that "God reigns!" and to bring this good news to the Bartimaeuses of life: to those in the streets, to the needy, the forgotten, the suffering, the brokenhearted.

Jesus is passing by here. He has stopped for us; he is calling out to us. He has stopped for us and is looking into our hearts. Does he see someone who is blind to his challenge and his invitation? Or does he see someone willing to follow him to bring good news to the impure and forgotten? Christ is calling out. Throw aside the mantle, follow him on the way, and be transformed in the following.

## SUGGESTIONS FOR WORSHIP

### Call to Worship

Your steadfast love, O LORD, extends to the heavens,
    your faithfulness to the clouds.
Your righteousness is like the mighty mountains,
    your judgments are like the great deep;
    you save humans and animals alike, O LORD.
How precious is your steadfast love, O God!
    All people may take refuge in the shadow of your wings.
They feast on the abundance of your house,
    and you give them drink from the river of your delights.
For with you is the fountain of life;
    in your light we see light (Ps. 36:5-9).

On this day the Lord calls us into God's presence that we may receive light from our darkness, and in that light, that we receive sight for our blindness. Come into the light of God's love.

### Prayer of Confession

We come before you, O Lord, and in your light we recognize our nakedness, our sinfulness, and our blindness. We ask your forgiveness for being blind to the pain and need that surrounds us. We ask your forgiveness for seeking to stay blind, so that we may live comfortably and unperturbed. In spite of ourselves, your voice has pierced our numbness, and your tears have rent our hearts. Let us never again be blinded to human need and human pain. Let us follow you on the Way of the Cross, and be faithful to your call to service, justice, and love for others. In Jesus' name we pray. Amen.

## Assurance of Pardon (Ps. 34:4, 8)

I sought the LORD, and [God] answered me. . . . O taste and see that the LORD is good; happy are those who take refuge in [God]!

## Benediction

And so we go out into the world, no longer blind but seeing. We go, no longer unfeeling, but caring. We go, no longer deaf, but hearing the cries of those in pain. May the Love of the Father, the Light of the Son, and the Power of the Holy Spirit live through us and for others. Shalom.

# Contributors

**Barbara Bate,** Director of Preaching Resources, United Methodist Church General Board of Discipleship, Nashville, Tennessee. Barbara, an active laywoman at Edgehill United Methodist Church in Nashville, has a thirteen-year-old daughter, two cats, and a piano she has played for many years—classical to gospel, Broadway to big band.

**Marsha Foster Boyd,** Assistant Professor of Pastoral Psychology, United Theological Seminary, Dayton, Ohio. An ordained minister of the African Methodist Episcopal Church, Marsha enjoys seeing her husband and daughter when she is not busy putting the finishing touches on her doctoral dissertation.

**Lynda Hyland Burris,** Pastor, Petaluma United Church of Christ, Petaluma, California. Lynda, a published poet, incorporates her love for drama and music into the creative worship of her church. At home she presides over a small menagerie of three very fluffy cats ("the furry burries") and one husband.

**Linda L. Clader,** Associate Professor of Homiletics, Church Divinity School of the Pacific, Berkeley, California. An Episcopal priest, Linda comes to preaching from a background in classical Greek and Roman literature. She is particularly interested in the way ancient epic and drama tell archetypal stories. Her favorite book is Homer's *Odyssey,* and her favorite color is red.

**Mary G. Graves,** Associate Pastor, Solana Beach Presbyterian Church, Solana Beach, California. Mary began her ministry in Christian camping and currently enjoys giving specialized leadership in Singles Ministry at the Solana Beach church. An avid runner, Mary thinks the scenery and the weather of the Solana Beach area (located near San Diego) may be the most beautiful in all of Presbyterianism.

**Mary Lin Hudson,** Assistant Professor of Homiletics and Worship, Memphis Theological Seminary, Memphis, Tennessee. An ordained minister in the Cumberland Presbyterian Church, Mary Lin loves fixing things—especially old houses. She plays the piano and sings (a little, she says) to accompany her bird, dog, three cats, and several fish.

**Nancy Lambing,** Pastor, of both Udall and Peck United Methodist Churches, Udall, Kansas. A pastor for the last seven years, Nancy enjoys church and family life (which includes a husband and two children). For relaxation, she reads; for exercise, she waterskis; and for renewal, she retreats to her sewing room.

**Loida Martell-Otero,** Associate Pastor, Iglesia Bautista Cristiana de Soundview, Bronx, New York. Loida is a veterinarian called out of the mountains of Puerto Rico. She collects penguins, coordinates a bilingual ministry, and has a great bunch of church kids who make her eyes shine.

**Alyce M. McKenzie,** Visiting Lecturer in Homiletics, Princeton Theological Seminary, Princeton, New Jersey. An ordained elder in The United Methodist Church, Alyce lives in Bucks County, Pennsylvania, with her husband and three children. She advocates for children's rights to health care and day care and is an avid reader of mystery fiction.

**Elizabeth Nordquist,** Associate Pastor, St. Peter's-by-the-Sea Presbyterian Church, Rancho Palos Verdes, California. "Mercifully," Elizabeth says, she is not a grandmother yet. But she does have a husband and two grown children and realizes that this means the stage is set. Working on her Doctor of Ministry degree takes all of what she used to think of as her spare time.

**Joan SalmonCampbell,** Pastor, St. Mark's Presbyterian Church, Cleveland, Ohio. The first clergywoman to be elected Moderator of the General Assembly of the Presbyterian Church (USA), Joan reports an excitement in her church about the use of the lectionary. It functions as a reminder of the global Church's common bonds.

**Mary J. Scifres,** Pastor, First United Methodist Church, Dearborn, Michigan. Mary is a pastor whose ministry receives not only the support of her congregation and her husband, but also of her feline "child." Gossip makes a habit of sitting next to Mary and talking nonstop while she writes her sermons.

**Nancy Hastings Sehested,** Pastor, Prescott Memorial Baptist Church, Memphis, Tennessee. Nancy, has been married for twenty-two years, has two daughters and loves mountain climbing. Her sermon composition is encouraged by the silent, steady presence of a "canine grace-note" named Duffy.

**Barbara Brown Taylor,** Rector, Grace-Calvary Episcopal Church, Clarkesville, Georgia. Barbara has published four collections of sermons, the latest of which is *Gospel Medicine*. Her book *The Preaching Life* addresses the life and faith of the baptized as they seek to be and speak the good news.

**Penny Zettler,** Pastor of Congregational Care, Friendship Church, Prior Lake, Minnesota, and Preaching Faculty Associate, Bethel Theological Seminary. Penny loves preaching, gardening, and cooking and is willing to share her secret salsa recipe.

# Scripture Index